Copywriting That Works:

Bright Ideas to Help You Inform, Persuade, Motivate and Sell!

Copywriting That Works:

Bright Ideas to Help You Inform, Persuade, Motivate and Sell!

Paul Lima

Published by

PAUL LIMA PRESENTS

www.paullima.com/books

Copywriting That Works:
Bright Ideas to Help You Inform, Persuade, Motivate and Sell!
Fourth Edition

Cover and interior design: Paul Lima. Copyright © 2011

Published by Paul Lima Presents – www.paullima.com/books

Manufactured in the U.S.A.

Published in Canada

Fourth Edition 2011

Library & Archives Canada/Bibliothèque & Archives Canada Data Main entry under title:

Copywriting That Works: Bright Ideas to Help You Inform, Persuade, Motivate and Sell!

Lima, Paul

ISBN: 978-0-9809869-7-6

1. Title

Contents

Introduction — *vii*

Chapter 1: Getting Started — *1*

Chapter 2: How the Ad Industry Works — *9*

Chapter 3: The Importance of Creativity — *13*

Chapter 4: Copywriting and W5 — *21*

Chapter 5: The Writing Process — *24*

Chapter 6: Target Market & Headlines — *31*

Chapter 7: The Tip of the Iceberg — *38*

Chapter 8: The Base of the Iceberg — *43*

Chapter 9: Headlines and Copy Blocks — *53*

Chapter 10: The Poetry of Copywriting — *62*

Chapter 11: Advertising's Environment — *70*

Chapter 12: From Branding to Hard Sell — *74*

Chapter 13: Writing Copy — *80*

Chapter 14: The Communications Process — *88*

Chapter 15: Direct Response Marketing — *93*

Chapter 16: Direct Response Sales Letter — *101*

Chapter 17: DRM in Action — *110*

Chapter 18: Brochure Writing Process — *120*

Chapter 19: Web-based DRM — *124*

Chapter 20: Search Engine Optimization — *131*

Chapter 21: Search Engine Pay Options — *135*

Chapter 22: Copywriting and Social Media — *140*

Chapter 23: Copywriting and Blogs — *147*

Chapter 24: Questions to Ask a Client — *152*

Chapter 25: Ad Bloopers — *154*

Chapter 26: Case Studies — *156*

Chapter 27: Appendices — *161*

Chapter 28: About the Author — *165*

Introduction

Welcome to *Copywriting That Works: Bright Ideas to Help You Inform, Persuade, Motivate and Sell!*—a book for those who want to understand the magic behind the voodoo known as advertising copywriting. If you want to master the craft of writing copy that informs, persuades, motivates, and/or sells, this book is for you. It will guide you through the process of producing copy that works—no matter your objective or target market. You will discover how to find your unique selling proposition, craft concepts that create desire, compose headlines that command attention, and write body copy that keeps readers interested and motivates them to take action.

All that you learn can be applied to writing newspaper and magazine ads, billboards, direct mail, brochures, email, web copy, and social media promotions. In short, this book will enable you to:

- Generate creative advertising ideas
- Translate ideas into concepts that hook your reader
- Increase your ability to write effective advertising copy
- Understand and apply the elements of successful print ads, direct response marketing, Google ads, website landing pages, and social media

When it comes to copywriting, this book is meant to get you started, point you in the right direction, and help you avoid common mistakes many beginners (and some veterans) make. I hope to inspire you, to give you options to pursue, and to help you create a solid foundation upon which you can build. Unlike many books on writing, this one does not promise to turn you into an overnight sensation—the creative director or senior copywriter at an award-winning agency. However, if you follow the hints, tips and techniques in this book, you will become an all-round better writer and a solid copywriter—whether you are writing copy for your own business or for clients.

I'd like to thank Leslie Smith (www.smithleslie.com), a freelance writer, editor, and business writing instructor, for editing several editions of this book. Her insights and comments have helped bring greater clarity and focus to the book.

Paul Lima
www.paullima.com

Chapter 1: Getting Started

While not ubiquitous, it feels as if advertising is everywhere—in newspapers and magazines, on radio, TV and the web, on billboards, in subway stations, on taxicabs. Even above urinals and on washroom cubicle doors.

Before you read this book and try the exercises in it, take a moment to think about your impressions of advertising and copywriting. Perhaps a good place to start would be with your definitions of advertising and copywriting. How would you define advertising? How would you define copywriting? When thinking about your impressions of advertising and copywriting, a list of questions may include:

- Why do companies, government agencies and not-for-profit organizations use advertising?
- Where and when do they advertise?
- What is the purpose of advertising?
- What does copywriting mean to you?
- Where do you see "copy?"
- How do you feel about advertising?
- What makes an advertisement effective? Ineffective? Is it different for print ads versus broadcast (radio and TV) commercials?
- Why are you reading this book? How do you plan to use it?

Advertising Defined

There are many definitions of advertising. Most of them are variations on a theme:

> Meant to draw public attention, advertising is the paid public promotion of a product, service, business, organization, or idea by an identified sponsor.

While the public frequently views advertising as encompassing all forms of promotional communication, most advertising practitioners limit it to paid communications conveyed by a mass medium, such as newspapers or TV. Direct marketing, such as direct mail, is a highly targeted form of advertising.

Advertising is distinguished from other forms of promotion or marketing—including publicity, public relations, personal selling and sales promotion.

The overall promotion or marketing mix elements include:

- **Advertising**: Print—magazine, newspaper, billboard, transit, point of sale (POS) and so on; Broadcast—radio and TV; Online—banner ads, pay-per-click ads, electronic newsletters, etc.
- **Direct Marketing**: Mail, Telephone, Email or Fax Broadcast
- **Public Relations**: Media Relations (Press Release, Press Kit), Publicity/Sponsorship
- **Sales Collateral**: Sales or Product/Services Brochure, Product Catalogue, Price List, Website
- **Guerrilla Marketing**: Social Engineering—in person or online
- **Direct Sales Force**

Copy is used in all forms of promotion (many salespeople follow scripts). In fact, copy is used in every major area of business, such as the writing of sales letters, brochures, business plans, websites, email, newsletters, employee communications, and so on. However, the use of copy in a document does not make the document an advertisement.

For the copy to be considered advertising copy, it must be part of a non-personal, paid communication that uses a particular medium to promote goods, services, companies, organizations, or ideas to the public or to a business audience.

The advertiser targets a specific business or consumer group, also known as the *target market*. Often the advertising aims for the target market's heart—though the head and the wallet are of vital interest to the advertiser.

> **Target Market** - A defined segment of the market that is the strategic focus of a business or marketing plan. The members of this segment possess common characteristics and a relative high propensity to purchase a particular product or service. Because of this, the members of this segment represent the greatest potential for sales volume and frequency. The target market is often defined in terms of geographic, demographic and psychographic characteristics.

The goal of advertising, generally, is to inspire action. Ad copy, however, has a hierarchical function. Before an ad (or ad campaign) can inspire action it must:

- Capture the *attention* of the target market
- Hold the *interest* of the target market
- Alter the target market's *attitude*

Then, and only then, can it motivate the target market to take *action*—an action that is defined by the company sponsoring the ad or the advertising campaign. That action, as we shall see, is not always "Buy now!"

> **Advertising Campaign**: A series of advertisements that share a single or similar theme or concept. Ads in campaigns may appear in different media across a specific period of time and use different words and images, but for the ads to be part of a campaign, its words and images must be related to a unifying theme.

While you could say that the main function of the ad is to motivate action (we will look at this more closely when we discuss the purpose of the ad), you must capture the *attention* of the target market first. If you do not make the reader, viewer or listener sit up and take notice, you will not be able to interest your audience. In other words, if you do not capture attention, then your audience will not read, view, listen to, or otherwise hang around to absorb your message. If you fail to interest your target market, you will not alter their attitude—move them from unaware to aware, from negative to positive, from positive to a true believer. And if you cannot alter (or reinforce) attitude, you cannot motivate readers or viewers to take action—as defined by the purpose of your ad.

The Role of the Copywriter

Can the copywriter do all of that? Given proper support by the graphic designer and media buyers, yes. It's not an easy task but, in many ways, that is what this entire book is about.

When it comes to advertising, copywriters produce the written or spoken elements of ads. It is the job of the copywriter to compose the language of the advertisement in such a way that it makes the promoted product or service desirable or memorable—at least as far as the target market is concerned. Although they are often involved in the larger creative issues, such as developing the *concept* or *hook* on which graphic artists, photographers and the directors of commercials hang their efforts, copywriters focus on the words.

Concept is Critical

For instance, IBM ran an ad for its ThinkPad notebook computers that portrayed a ThinkPad with a deployed airbag. The headline/subhead read:

> The IBM active protection system is like an airbag for your notebook.
>
> It protects your data against accidents when you are on the road.

What is the concept? *Protection.* Why protection?

People who buy portable computers are often concerned about dropping them and losing data, or having someone steal them and access their data. So the concept—protection—appeals to the target market.

To illustrate protection, IBM uses a *metaphor*. Protecting data on the ThinkPad is compared to something most people understand: airbags. Can you see how the airbag metaphor and the image (a ThinkPad with an airbag deployed from its screen) spring from that concept?

Can you see how the concept itself is related to the concerns of the target market, the mobile businessperson?

Airbags are found in cars. Cars move. The target market is mobile. Airbags offer protection. Notebooks have data that needs to be protected. So the copy and the image, working in harmony, convey the concept or hook.

> **Concept**: The general idea behind a slogan, pitch or advertising campaign. A general statement of the idea behind the advertisement.

Without a concept or hook, you can still have an ad. However, you will have a poor ad that does not resonate with your target market. You may also have a difficult time creating and writing an ad that does not start with a concept, because, as you will see, the hook or concept lets you create a *theme* that runs through your ad and connects the elements of the ad to the ad's objective and target market.

In short, the images and words used in the ad all spring from the concept. The concept is the copywriter's best friend.

Purpose of Advertising

Notice, I've written a lot about advertising and copywriting without mentioning the "S" word: *Selling.* Many people believe the purpose of advertising is to sell. But how many ads have motivated you to buy? How often have you seen an ad and immediately bought something? Not often, I'm sure. Otherwise, you would be shopping non-stop.

While the purpose of an ad can be to sell immediately, ads are often used to plant seeds that germinate the next time a consumer is shopping or in need of something. They do this by educating, informing, and building brand awareness or positioning—associating a particular image or emotion (one that appeals to the target market) with a brand, product or service.

> **Positioning**: Orchestrating an organization's offering or a product's image to occupy a unique and valued place in the customer's mind relative to competitive offerings. A product or service can be positioned based on an attribute or benefit, use or application, user, class, price or quality, image or emotional association.
>
> **Brand Awareness**: The likelihood that a particular brand will be thought of and recognized (favourably) when consumers think of the product category in which the brand operates.

Ads can also be used to remind consumers to fill a *need*, such as to quench thirst. However, most ads sell products for which there is no need, even ads, as we shall see, that purport to fulfill a need such as the need to quench one's thirst. Where there is no need, it is the job of the ad to create *desire* for the product or to create a desire for a particular emotional fulfillment and then *associate* the fulfillment of that emotion with the product.

Can Ads Sell You Something You do not Need?

Of course they can! When was the last time you *needed* chocolate? You might *desire* or *crave* it, but you do not *need* it. You might crave the sexual allure (emotional need) you see in many chocolate ads and you might associate eating chocolate with sexual fulfillment. However, you do not *need* chocolate. Look at this slogan once used by Cadbury Caramilk:

> Discover the secret to pleasure.

Remember, we are talking about chocolate here. It seems that advertisers are trying to convince people that chocolate is better than sex! But, the fact is, you don't need it. (Chocolate, that is.)

> **Slogan**: A short, memorable advertising phrase. Examples include "Coke Is It," "Just Do It" and "Don't Leave Home Without It." When a product or company uses a slogan consistently, the slogan can become an important element of product identification and the public's perception of the product.

Maslow's Hierarchy of Needs

Let's look at the role of advertising within *Maslow's Hierarchy of Needs*.

Maslow's Hierarchy of Needs
Self Actualization: *Fully realizing one's individual human potential*
Esteem *Honoured, regarded highly*
Love *Affection and belonging*
Safety *Physical and psychological*
Physiological *Survival needs such as food, air and water*

The noted humanistic psychologist, Abraham Maslow, claimed that human beings are motivated by unsatisfied needs. He placed these needs within a hierarchy. Working up from the bottom of the hierarchy, individuals must satisfy a lower need before they are motivated to fulfill higher needs. For instance, the need for safety cannot be satisfied until the physiological need (food, water) is met. The need for love cannot be satisfied until the need for safety is met, and so on.

Most individuals in North America have satisfied physiological and safety needs. Some, certainly not all, have satisfied the need for love. That leaves the majority of us trying to fulfill our need for love and almost all of us working on esteem and self-actualization. Love, esteem and self-actualization are three difficult needs to satisfy. That is where advertising steps in. It promotes products and services meant to help us fill these gaps, to help us believe we are satisfying our need for love, esteem or self-actualization by ... shopping.

What about Business-to-Business Advertising?

You could argue that business-to-business (B2B) advertising satisfies concrete needs—the need to save time and money or to work more productively, for instance. Then you would have to ask if we truly have a need for business. If so, which of Maslow's Hierarchy of Needs does business or capitalism satisfy?

While a discussion of that nature goes well beyond the scope of this book, suffice it to say that we do not necessarily need all or much of what is advertised. Even hard-nosed business people make emotional buying decisions. Do banks *need* tall towers with their logos on them? Do corporate lawyers *need* their rich mahogany desks and expensive Montblanc pens? It's tough to make a pure business case for such expenditures. However, if we stopped buying, the entire economic foundation of Western Civilization would collapse.

So, like it or not, advertising has an important role to play in our society. In fact, one might be tempted to say that, as a society, we need advertising.

To become aware of the devices copywriters use to appeal to so-called needs, analyze ads. Examine them and ask: What *need* does the ad seem to appeal to? How does it do this? Why does it do this?

You might be surprised by how often the ad is not appealing to a concrete need, even when it claims to be doing so. Instead, it is masking a desire or craving as a need. Take, for instance, Oh Henry! chocolate bars. At the time of writing this book, there were Oh Henry! ads that posed a question and answered it:

Oh Hungry?

Oh Henry!

On the surface, it looks as if the ad is appealing to the need to fulfill hunger. But do we need chocolate, sugar, nuts and whatever other ingredients go into this chocolate bar? This ad may seem as if it is saying to the consumer: *You get hungry. Here is a quick and easy way to satisfy your hunger.* However, eating an apple is a quick, easy, (and nutritional) way of satisfying hunger.

What is this line really doing? Oh Henry! is co-opting Maslow's Hierarchy of Needs (in this case the need to satisfy hunger) and turning the need into a desire or craving for sugar and chocolate. *Desires* and *cravings* are not *needs*.

I don't want to pick on chocolate. We can say similar things about perfume, beer, designer label clothing, monster homes, Ferraris, Post-It Notes, electronic lemon peelers, any fast food, iPods, even computers and the Internet, and so on.

Some might argue that certain products fulfill needs such as love (you wear perfume to help you attract a mate), esteem (you can afford a Ferrari, you must be important), or self-actualization (you work hard; look at all you can afford; you must feel fulfilled). However, if advertisers focused solely on fulfilling legitimate needs, many companies would be out of business.

Into that reality—the reality that most of what is advertised is not needed; it may be desired or useful, but it is not needed—steps you, the copywriter!

Chapter 2: How the Ad Industry Works

It is difficult to describe how the adverting industry works, as there arc so many components to it.

Beyond creative, the ad industry also requires media buyers to buy ad space and airtime, account representatives to source clients and hold their hands as campaigns are developed, plus a host of others who make the industry tick.

Most large ad agencies have creative directors, graphic artists and writers. They tend to contract out the production of broadcast commercials. Many agencies contract out other elements of ad production—including graphic art, photography and writing.

Some companies have in-house agencies that develop some or all of their advertising. Again, the production of broadcast commercials is generally contracted out. Some in-house agencies may also contract out other elements of ad production. To land work with an ad agency—either as an employee or as a freelancer—you need a portfolio or body of work that demonstrates your creative *thinking* and *writing* (or artistic ability if you are looking for a gig as a graphic designer or photographer).

100 Ideas = One Concept

Some creative directors and copywriters start into a project looking for one big idea, concept or hook on which to hang an ad. This is a myopic approach to advertising. At a minimum, clients expect three creative concepts. (This does not always apply to many small- and medium-sized businesses on tight budgets and tight schedules. Sadly, because they move so quickly and pinch pennies, they waste much of their marketing dollars.)

As any ad agency will tell you, only the cleverest ideas are presented to the client. Often, the client and agency will brainstorm variations on the ideas. The client may even reject all ideas and ask the agency to go back to the drawing-board. It is the nature of the industry. It is also, some would say, the nature of creative process. But more on creativity and the creative process later in the book.

When is comes to creativity, what is the client looking for? Let's stick with beer (something, one could argue, we could all do without—at least in terms of needs). We are talking Bud, a beer that tastes like almost every other mass-produced beer on the market. We are talking a product with no unique selling proposition (USP). There is nothing that differentiates it from the competition—other than its advertising (and maybe price, if it is on sale).

> **USP**: The proposition or selling point (feature, benefit or *advantage*) that makes your product, service or brand *unique*, or *differentiates* it from the competition.

Domino's all but took over the delivered pizza market with their USP:

Fresh, hot pizza delivered in 30 minutes or less, guaranteed!

Domino's did not even promise that the pizza would taste good. Of course, the USP has since been copied by many competitors, as is often the case with USPs that work, rendering it less than unique. So today's USP may not be the USP you use tomorrow.

Anyone who grew up feasting on M&M's can tell you its USP is:

M&M's melt in your mouth, not in your hands.

Does "melts in your mouth..." sound more like a slogan? It became a slogan. It was first used as a headline. It was also what differentiated M&Ms from other candies, hence it was a USP.

Again, USPs are often co-opted by the competition and must change when they are no longer unique. Anacin offered "fast, fast relief." Now almost every pain medicine acts "fast." Colgate used to say, "Cleans your breath as it cleans your teeth." Try to find toothpaste that does not do that today. In fact, try to find a mouth rinse that does not clean your teeth!

When it comes to advertising a beer like Bud, what is the client looking for? Ads that capture the attention and hold the interest of viewers (preventing them from reaching for the remote channel changer). Ads that are amusing or, better still, hilarious. Ads that are worth watching more than once. Ads that are memorable. Ads that, when you are in the beer store contemplating which brand to buy, sneak up behind you, hit you on the head, and make you say, "Um ... Bud Light, please."

No easy task, that. Hence, the need for 100 creative concepts before one strikes creative gold—the ad that makes it to the Super Bowl.

Test First

Sometimes, it takes the development of 100 creative concepts before you can find that one brilliant idea. Ironically, in this all-too-subjective world of advertising, 100 concepts can lead to one idea that falls flat.

Time and budget do not always allow for the development of 100 ideas. They do not always allow for the opportunity to test-market ads. At a minimum, a creative director (or copywriter, if the copywriter is wearing the creative director's hat) should come up with three concepts (along with proposed headlines and images) for the client. These concepts should keep in mind the purpose of the ad and the target market (see Chapter 7).

Once a concept is selected, the headline, image and body copy should be revised and finalized. If possible, the final ad should be tested. The test can be as simple as showing the ad to current or prospective clients and asking them a few questions to determine how they feel about the ad, what they think about the ad, and what they think the ad is asking them to do. The test can be as complex as bringing together a focus group representing the target market and having folks in white coats hide behind one-way mirrors taking notes, as a professional facilitator leads the group through a series of questions and conversations related to the ad or ads (if testing a number of concepts).

Creativity and Brainstorming

How does an ad agency come up with 100 concepts (or even three)? It is a creative endeavour. Whether there is one person working alone or a team working together, *brainstorming* forms the foundation of this creative endeavour. Brainstorming is a technique for generating, refining and developing ideas. While brainstorming can be undertaken by individuals, brainstorming is most effective when undertaken by a group. However, many writers do their brainstorming in isolation. They sit, ponder and mull. They look out the window, hoping that inspiration will strike.

When I worked as the senior copywriter for Central Advertising, the in-house advertising agency for Radio Shack Canada (now The Source), I had to keep a timesheet because the agency charged back time spent on a job to the department that commissioned the work. The timesheet was broken down into 10-minute increments and a code was applied to each increment or block of time. One of our codes, 2-8, signified "non-productive" time. In other words, when I used 2-8 on my timesheet, my time could not be charged back to another department

As you can imagine, the advertising staff did not want to use 2-8 on timesheets. But when you are brainstorming, which might involve looking out a window, or looking at the ceiling or picking lint off your slacks, you can appear rather unproductive.

Every now and then, the Director of Advertising would stick his head into my cubicle and catch me doing something that looked a lot like counting holes in ceiling tiles. "Ah," he'd say, "I see a lot of 2-8 going on today."

The fact is, many people who are not involved in creating or who aren't part of the creative process do not understand the need to think and ponder or mull. However, instead of looking out windows for inspiration you can use a variety of creative writing exercises to spark your creativity.

> **Creativity:** The experience of thinking, reacting and working in an imaginative and idiosyncratic way, characterized by a high degree of innovation, originality and divergent thinking—the ability to bring forth ideas, concepts, products, artwork, and so on.

Creativity is about producing new ideas or combining old ideas in a way that produces something new. Only constrained by imagination, creativity starts with an idea or vision (the *Eureka*! moment). Then the creator has to organize the concept and describe it to a client or production team. If the description is accepted and/or understood, the idea can move to prototyping or production.

But how do you spark creativity? Before we look at the specifics of copywriting, I want you to experience several creative writing exercises.

The exercises in Chapter 4 are meant to spark your creativity, to help you create in as free a style as possible. And they beat counting ceiling tiles, which was I was often doing as I waited for inspiration to strike. Instead of waiting for inspiration, you are going to go hunting for it, using brainstorming as your main weapon.

Brainstorming, or this ability to think freely, helps spark *Eureka!* moments, especially when deadlines loom. Later in the book, we will apply many of these creative exercises to specific copywriting tasks.

Chapter 3: The Importance of Creativity

My internal critic/censor is Mr. Conron, the grade five teacher who would not give me a pen (he made me use a pencil all year) because I could not spell well or write neatly.

Is it "*i*" before "*e*" or "*e*" before "*i*" except after "*c*" or when writing "*weird*" because that word is just ... well, *wierd*? Of course, my writing was messy because I could not spell! When you don't know if it's "*i*" before "*e*" you make a chubby "*i*" and a skinny "*e*" and put the dot right in the middle, hoping to fool the teacher!

Anyway, Mr. Conron wielded his red marker like the sword of Zorro, gleefully cutting huge red gashes across my mistakes. He never once commented on content or creativity. He just slashed at mistakes, as if perfect spelling and grammar are what writing is all about. There was no room for art or craft, just correct spelling and grammar. Oh, and neatness.

I battle Mr. Conron whenever I attempt to master the creative art of writing. When he rears his ugly head, I say, "Get thee behind me, Satan!" And I keep on writing—through typos and grammatical errors. Through incomplete sentences and incorrect words. I write until I have finished an error-filled first draft and then I laugh in his face. Because I have learned something about writing: Writing is a process. First you create. Then you correct. Mr. Conron (and Word's automatic grammar and spell check) be dammed!

Even before you create, there are steps you need to take to become a more effective and efficient writer. However, before we look at the writing process in detail, answer me this: You, too, have an internal censor. Who is it? Take a moment. Identify your critic/censor. Name him or her. Give him/her a nickname (like *Satan*). Place your thumb on the tip of your nose and wiggle your fingers at him/her. Go on. Do it. Say your critic's name (or names!) out loud and thumb your nose at *your* Mr. Conron....

There! Doesn't that feel better?

Now ... pick up a pen. Find a sheet of paper. And write about your internal censor/critic. Write without stopping or correcting yourself. Screw spelling, grammar and neatness. Just write, write, write. Write as if you were freefalling— falling from an airplane without a parachute.

Nothing can stop you. Not grammar. Not spelling. Not Mr. Conron. Take five or ten minutes and write, write, write.... *On your mark ... Get set ... Go!*

How to Overcome Your Mr. Conron

Welcome back. Hope you are feeling okay... First, understand that writing is a *process.* Mistakes are part of the process. In the process, there is a time to *create* and a time to *revise.* If you do not follow the process, Mr. C. will trip you up every time. He will get you *revising* or *editing* when you should be *creating.* He will cause you to waste time editing work that is not even at the first-draft stage. He will have you feeling frustrated and stupid.

Writing is difficult enough without Satan squeezing the last ounce of fun out of what should be a challenging but enjoyable creative art or craft. I use several creative writing exercises to bypass Mr. C. They help me focus on the creative aspect of the work. I save dotting the *i*'s and crossing the *t*'s for the last stage of the process—editing—and relegate Mr. C. to a small (but important) role as *editor.* In short, I lock him in a cupboard, feed him nothing, and only use him when I need him.

Before we look at the right brain, or creative, exercises in this book, chew on a few words for thought:

> It took me my whole life to learn how to paint like a child again.
> – *Pablo Picasso*

> Never look at a reference book while doing a first draft. You want to write a story? Fine. Put away your dictionary, your encyclopaedias, your World Almanac and your thesaurus.... You think you might have misspelled a word? Okay, so here's your choice: either look it up in the dictionary to make sure you have it right—and break your train of thought—or spell it phonetically

and correct it later. Why not? Do you think the word is going to go away? When you sit down to write, write. Don't do anything else except go to the bathroom, and only do that if it absolutely cannot be put off.
– *Stephen King*

Do you see what these words are saying? When you are creating, you must overcome your inhibitions and internal censors. You must be as free as a child. In short, *when you are creating, spelling and grammar do not count.*

There will be time for correcting later, once you have a concept and have completed a first draft. After all, who do you show the first draft to? (*To whom do you show your first draft?*) Nobody! Who cares if there are *tpyos*? Fix them later.

If you are working in a word-processing program like Word and you have your spell checker and grammar checker turned on, you are inviting Mr. Conron to inhibit your creativity. You are seeing and correcting so-called mistakes as you write—before you complete your first draft. In doing so, you are wasting time and losing your creative train of thought. Brain-storming, pre-writing exercises and the first draft are for your eyes only.

With that in mind, *turn off spell check and grammar check and get creating.* Try these exercises using pen and paper, unless otherwise indicated. There is something formal about neat rows of letters and words on the computer screen. They just seem to cry out for revision when you should be focused on creation! So use pen and paper for the exercises.

Right-brain Writing and Pre-writing Exercises

Below are several right-brain (the creative side of the brain) writing exercises.

Freefall

Freefall has been called "writing without a parachute" or "stream of consciousness." It's ideally done using pen and paper rather than on the computer. With freefall, there is no goal or destination. You start without a beginning and do not have to end anywhere in particular. Just jot down the first thought that pops into your mind, followed by the next and then the next and then the next.... Write quickly, without stopping to edit or revise.

In other words, follow the stream of consciousness as it meanders through your mind. Write without censoring yourself, until you reach what feels like an end. Or not. Give yourself at least five minutes, if not more. If you find yourself stopping, keep the pen moving on the page. Use ellipses (...) or squiggles (or whatever marks you feel like using) until you tap back into the stream of consciousness and are off and writing again.

Experience freefall. Use a separate sheet of paper and just ... start ... writing! Try two five-minute freefalls. Take a short break between each one. Go....

Directed Freefall

Directed Freefall works like freefall, only you are given (or produce) an opening line to help direct your creation. However, as with freefall, there is no goal or destination. Simply write as freely as possible, without censoring yourself. See where your writing takes you. Here are a several opening lines that you can use to kick-start your directed freefall:

- In the beginning was....
- On the day that I was born....
- Travelling across the city by foot....
- In the old woman's face, I saw....
- It all ended the day....
- In the town where I grew up....
- Once upon a time....
- It came upon a midnight's eve....

Pick a line. Jot it down, and freefall from there. Take five minutes and just do nothing else but write, write, write.... When your freefall seems to have come to an end, pick another line and go again...

> **Freefall hint**: Before you begin writing anything important, freefall for five minutes. It helps clear the mind so you can focus on your task. Also, you might find inspiration related to your work.

Clustering

Now we're going to try clustering. A form of brainstorming (also called mind mapping or word association), clustering lets you brainstorm in a visual manner.

When clustering, you jot down (using a specific method) all the words you *associate* with a given topic, keyword or phrase.

The goal is to get down on paper all you know and associate with your keyword. Once again, work quickly—without censoring yourself. That means you might jot down some words or phrases that seem "silly." However, you never know where these so-called silly words will lead. So, whatever comes up, goes down!

How do You Cluster?

When given your keyword or phrase:

1. Jot it down in the middle of a blank page, underline it and circle it.
2. Draw a short line (more like a long dash) from your keyword and jot down the first word or phrase that comes to mind.
3. Circle that word or phrase (optional).
4. Draw a short line from that word or phrase, and jot down the next word or phrase that comes to mind.
5. Repeat until you come to the end of the cluster string of associated words (in other words, until you go blank).
6. Return to your keyword.
7. Moving quickly, draw a short line from your keyword and jot down the next word or phrase that comes to mind.
8. Circle that word or phrase, draw a short line from that word or phrase and carry on....

How many cluster strings should you create? It is up to you. The goal is to move as quickly as possible, without censoring, so you can get down as many words or phrases as possible that you associate with your keyword.

Why do you do this? Because it beats looking out the window waiting for inspiration to strike.

Clustering and freefalling are active forms of inspiring creative ideas. Also, as you will see, solid ad copy contains words and phrases related to the concept or hook behind the ad. You are, in effect, mining for words and phrases that will help you develop your ad theme.

If your concept (keyword) appeals to your target market, so will many of your cluster words. Used in ads, words that appeal to your target market are like landmarks. They help the target market identify with the product or service you are advertising and keep the target market interested or engaged in your ad.

Below is an example of clustering based on the keyword: <u>clustering</u>. Review the sample before you try a few of your own based on the keywords provided.

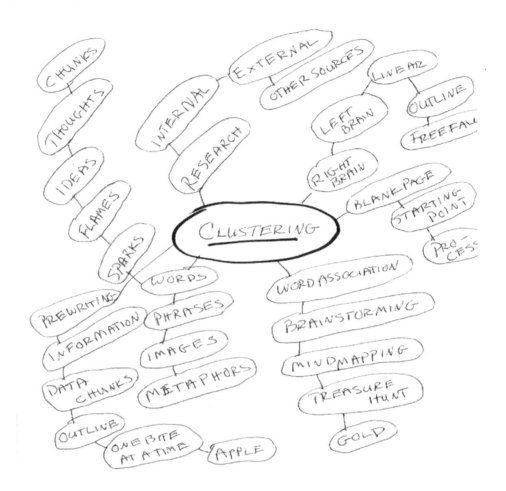

Here are several keywords you can use to kick-start your clustering:

- Apple
- Help
- Writing
- Summer (or any season you wish to use)
- Money
- Chocolate
- Mother (or Father or any sibling)

Before you read on, try clustering several times using a couple of the above words. Cluster for about five minutes each time, or work until your clustering exercise feels complete.

Cluster/Freefall Combo

Clustering is an excellent pre-writing exercise. It can be used to fuel your freefall. Once you have completed a cluster (a cluster is complete when it feels as if it is finished), flip into freefall, and write without stopping. However, if you find yourself slowing down or running dry, glance quickly at your cluster to spark your writing.

Using one of the words above or below, try a cluster/freefall combination:

- Home
- Mother
- Blue sky
- Last night
- Hunger
- Travel
- Fear

Notes on Clustering

You can use clustering to help you write anything once you have defined the *type of document* you are producing, *your target audience* and *your purpose*. For example, what you produce when clustering the word "Me" would change in relation to the *type of document* you are producing, *your target audience* and *your purpose* for each of these documents:

- Autobiography, childhood reminiscence or personal essay
- Business bio for a website or speaker's introduction
- Cover letter and resume

Could there be some overlap in your clustering? For sure. But given a direction (by defining the type of document you are producing, your target audience and your purpose) your clustering will shift into the appropriate gear—as long as you do not censor yourself.

Try multiple clusters for one project. Before writing a cover letter or resume, for example, cluster *Me*, *Education*, *Work Experience*, *Hobbies*, *Passion*, *Career Objective* and *Job Title* (the actual title of the job you are applying for).

Apply the results of your brainstorming to your cover letter and resume. Clustering these keywords will also help you prepare for your interview.

Chapter 4: Copywriting and W5

After doing right-brain creative work, you can get focused by going linear. To help you move from right-brain to left-brain thinking when faced with a copywriting project, ask yourself the kinds of questions a journalist would ask before writing an article. Ask yourself the W5 questions—Who, What, Where, When, Why (and sometimes How).

Get the answers down on paper before you begin to write. That way, when faced with an ad-writing project, you will be working from your *creative* side plus your *linear* notes.

Once you are given a product to write about, complete some of the right-brain exercises, such a freefall and clustering. Once you have done that, answer the questions below before you start to write your copy:

- Who is advertising?
- Whom are you advertising to? Who is your target?
- Who is the end user—consumer or business?
- Who are the early adopters and primary influencers? (Those most likely to buy a new product first and those most likely to influence others to try it.)
- What are you advertising? (Product, service or cause.)
- What are you advertising? (Actual name.)
- What are the features and benefits associated with the product?
- What need and/or desire does the product fulfill?
- What need and/or desire should you create and associate with the product?
- Why does the target market need/want/desire the product?
- How does the product or service fulfill the need/want/desire?
- What makes this product different from its competition?
- How does the target market acquire the product or service?
- What action, if any, do you want the target market to take upon reading (hearing/viewing) this ad?
- Why should they take it?

- What incentive (if any) are you offering to induce action?
- When does the incentive to action expire?
- Where does your target market go to take action?
- When can/should they do it? How?
- Where is the product or service available?
- When is the product or service available?
- What guarantee is there that the product will live up to expectations generated by the ad?
- How do you want the target market to feel after reading/hearing/viewing your ad?
- "What's in it for me?" (That's your target market asking.)

Most ads will answer some or all of these questions. It depends on the purpose of the ad, as we shall see. (Direct Response Marketing, which is meant to sell, will usually answer most, or all, of these questions.) However, as the copywriter, you should know the answers to the questions before you begin to write so that you can consciously decide what to put in and what to leave out of your copy.

Why do This Pre-writing?

Why ask these questions? Why not just write? Your goal is to create effective ads—ads that cut through the clutter of all the other ads out there. To do that, you need a powerful hook. To create that, you need knowledge and information. And options! In fact, there is even more information—the *marketing strategy*—you need to gather before you write. (We will review the marketing strategy—the base of the copywriting iceberg—in Chapter 8.)

How to Cut Through the Clutter

Your ad has to *AIAA*—capture *Attention*, hold *Interest*, influence *Attitude* and call for *Action*. If it doesn't capture your target market's *attention*, how will you create awareness of the brand, product, service or company you are promoting? But once you capture your target market's attention, your ad must hold the reader's *interest* if it is to develop, reinforce, or change your target market's *attitude*, the way your audience *feels* about the promoted product. Most purchase decisions, even many business purchase decisions, are emotional ones. If you can't influence attitude, how are you going to sell anything?

Finally, your ad has to motivate *action*. It's one thing to capture someone's attention and make someone aware of your brand and associate with it positive thoughts or feelings; it's quite another to motivate someone to act.

Try doing all that in a creative vacuum. Not easy. Try doing it without answers to key questions. Not at all easy. *And try doing it without a process*—a formal approach to writing. Extremely difficult.

Your job then, as we shall see, is to answer the linear or W5 questions, to review the marketing strategy, and then to apply creative brainstorming techniques so that you can develop a concept or hook on which to hang your copy (and image, if you are producing both the image and the copy, or if you are responsible for suggesting images to the creative director or ad designer).

Then you write with target market and purpose in mind.

Chapter 5: The Writing Process

Writing is a process. Most of us get hung up on correct spelling and grammar. That inhibits the process. Spelling and grammar count (although copywriters often break the rules for effect). But spelling and grammar are the last elements of the process. Preparation and planning come first. You become more effective and efficient if you follow the writing process. As one study found:

- **Efficient writers** spend 40% of their time planning (preparation, research and organization), 25% writing and 35% revising.

- **Less-efficient writers** spend more time overall on projects and distribute their time differently: 20% planning, 60% writing (tinkering, writing, tinkering), and 20% revising, tinkering, revising.

It may seem ironic to say you can become more efficient if you spend more time up front. However, the time you invest in planning pays dividends when it comes time to write and revise. Planning is your road map. If you plan a trip, you are more likely to reach your destination. You can still meander. However, if your meandering takes you nowhere, no problem. You will find it easier to get back on track because you have a plan, a road map and a process.

The Writing Process Includes

- **Planning**
  - Determine your topic
  - Establish your purpose
  - Identify and know your audience
  - Determine your scope (degree of detail required)
  - Select the appropriate medium

- **Research**
  - Brainstorm to determine what you know
  - Conduct research (background reading, Internet research, interviews) to gather what you need to know
  - Take organized notes

- **Organization**
  - Outline your points (topics) in the order in which they should be presented
  - Create and integrate visuals, if required
  - Consider layout and design

- **Writing**
  - Select appropriate point of view—first person (I), second person (you), third person (he, she, they)
  - Write a title (or headline and/or subhead)
  - Adopt appropriate style and tone
  - Use effective sentence and paragraph construction
  - Write an introduction and conclusion (for longer documents)
  - Write from topic point to topic point
  - Complete your first draft

- **Revision, Editing (proofreading)**
  - Check for completeness and accuracy
  - Check for coherence, clarity, conciseness and sentence variety
  - Eliminate jargon and clichés
  - Eliminate grammar problems and spelling mistakes
  - Share your document for feedback, or test it (if possible)

Planning

Establish your purpose or objective. Knowing your purpose will help you to conduct focused research, to include appropriate information, and to adopt a suitable writing tone.

Ask yourself: Why am I writing this document? To inform, educate, persuade, demonstrate how-to's, facilitate a decision, or recommend a course of action? For some other reason? What action do I want my audience to take? What do they need to know before they can act? What incentives can I offer them to act?

Identify your audience. Are you writing to peers, superiors, subordinates, customers, suppliers, other stakeholders or a mixed audience? What is (are) your audience's expectation(s)? Do you need to know anything about your audience's age, income, education, occupation, profession, state of mind and/or health, gender, marital status, sexual orientation, ethnicity, interests, political/religious persuasion...? This information will help you conduct focused research, include appropriate information in the document, and adopt a suitable writing tone.

Determine your scope. What depth and breadth of detail do you need to cover the subject, fulfill your purpose and meet your audience's expectation(s)?

Select the appropriate medium. As the nature of your medium changes, so too does the nature of your message. Are you writing an email message, sending a fax, writing a letter, creating a web page or producing a video? Are you writing a case study, a detailed report, a technical manual, a request for quote (RFQ)? Are you producing an advertisement for a newspaper or magazine, website, TV or radio broadcast?

Imagine trying to write without knowing what you are writing about, whom you are writing for, or the purpose of the document. Difficult to imagine, isn't it? However, many people do not produce a planning checklist, or they produce a mental checklist that does not include all the required elements. Then they wonder why they get lost in unfocused research or have a difficult time writing.

You can work through the outlined writing process elements by asking yourself the "W" questions: Who, What, Where, When and Why. No matter what you're writing, you can improve your writing significantly if you answer the "W" questions before you put pen to paper or hands to keyboard.

Before you start writing an ad (or any other document), supplement your planning by asking:

- Whom am I writing for (target audience or target market)?
- What am I writing about (subject)?
- Why am I writing (purpose)?
- What action (desired outcome) do I want to occur?
- Who takes the action?
- When and where should the action take place?
- How does/should it happen?
- How can I motivate the action?

Research

Research internally. Jot down on paper all you know and all you need to know about your subject or the product or service you are writing about. Identify knowledge gaps to help focus your research. If you possess all the required knowledge, interview yourself before you write! Try Clustering as a means of accomplishing this.

Research externally. Do background reading, Internet searches, interviews. Fill your knowledge gap(s) by conducting purposeful research.

Take organized notes. Use separate sheets or files for each significant research topic. This helps to develop your outline further.

Organization

Outline your ideas (in relation to your medium). Your outline enables you to move swiftly, from point to point, in the right direction. Think of it this way: For long documents (say 2,000 words), you can attempt to fill ten blank pages or you can produce a 10-point outline and write 10 shorter sections. Which seems simpler to you?

Your ad outline would include all the copy points you want to hit, in the order in which you want to write about them. You might not produce a formal outline for an ad that is going to be nothing more than an image, headline, slogan and website address. However, you will discover that outlines are critical for longer Direct Response Marketing (DRM) pieces such as direct mail and website landing pages. But don't ignore short outlines. An outline will make you a more effective and efficient writer, whether you are writing copy blocks of 25 words to several hundred words or more.

The objective is to know where you are going before you head out on the journey. You want to get down in point form each place (copy point) you will visit (write about) before you head off on your journey (start to write).

Do you want to see an outline in action? Look at the chapter headings for this book. They were all written before the text was written. Did the names of some of the chapters change as the book was being written? Yes. Did some chapters get broken in two? Yep. Were a few chapters shifted around? Actually, no. But it could have happened.

If that does not seem like much of an outline, look at the subheadings in each of the chapters. They were almost all in place before I began to write. I produced the outlines (there were several outline drafts) after completing planning and research.

I had an outline but there were several digressions and meanderings as I wrote. A few led nowhere and were deleted. Others were incorporated into the text. So, an outline does not stifle creativity and improvisation. It allows for it.

Create and integrate visuals, if required. Do you require photos, charts, graphs or graphics to illustrate points? Plan to source or create them and include them in your document.

Consider layout and design. Graphic artists design advertisements. They work with illustrators and photographers. However, the copywriter can often suggest graphics. The headline can inspire the visuals, if written before the layout is done—but the execution of the layout is best left up to professionals.

In some writing, layout and design are not important elements. An email message, for instance, may be written in plain text with no subheads. If, however, you are producing a document that is more than one page long, consider using headings, subheadings, bullet points and other simple layout elements to make it easier for your audience to read and understand. If you are producing a publication (newsletter or magazine) or an ad, bring in a graphic designer.

Writing

Select an appropriate point of view (POV). Should you use first person (*I*), second person (*you*) or third person (*he, she, they*)? Seldom do you see ads in first person, unless someone is giving a testimonial. Even then, they will use second person (*you*) as well.

Perhaps something like:

> The Filibuster 5000 changed my life for the better. It will change yours too. It brought me happiness beyond compare and I used to be a grumpy old man. Imagine what it can do for you....

Ads frequently use second person as a way of personalizing the ad, as a way of trying to make one-on-one contact with the reader through mass media:

> Aren't you glad you use Dial? Don't you wish everyone did?

Copy is often written in third person as well, particularly catalogue copy:

> Jockey Women's Medium-support Underwire Padded Bra. Seamless straps have ¾" longer adjustment to allow for in-between sizing. Cup and sides designed to help avoid overflow and ride up. Nylon-LYCRA elastin microfibre. Adjustable straps and back hook closure.

To help select POV, ask yourself: "Who's talking?" Is the advertiser talking to the target market? If so, the writer would most likely use "you" but might also use third person (most likely in catalogue copy).

Is it an existing customer talking to the target market? The customer might use "I" to tell his or her story, but "you" to make the ad appear personal—as if the customer were talking directly to the target market.

Is the anti-target market speaking? Sometimes ads will let a spokesperson who is the opposite of the target market speak. He/she may address others who would not buy the product, or may admonish the target market for desiring the product. In a quirky way (opposites in advertising are alike) this can be an effective appeal to the target market. Again, "you" is the POV of choice.

Are two people talking to each other? They could be two members of the target market, or one member of the target market and one anti-TM. They could be an existing customer and a prospect (member of the target market) that needs convincing. They would use "you" in talking to each other, and in that way reach the reader who is represented by one of the characters in the ad.

Adopt appropriate style and tone. Review your purpose, audience, scope and medium to determine if you should be casual, friendly, business-familiar or strictly business. Also, determine if you should be objective (presenting facts with no opinion) or subjective (expressing an opinion based on the evidence). Ads can range from casual to strictly business. The more business-like the ad, the more it projects an air of objectivity. But make no mistake about it, they are all subjective.

Use effective sentence and paragraph construction. When it comes to ad copy, "effective" may mean breaking some of the rules of grammar. For instance, you have probably been told that you cannot start a sentence with *and, but* or *because*. Or that complete sentences need a subject, verb and object. Poppycock! Why? Because. And that's all I'll say. But if you want more information, read on.

Vary your sentence length and style so your copy does not become monotonous.

> This is a simple sentence. On the other hand, this sentence, which is longer and uses clauses, is more complex.

The sentence mix should depend on your target market, copy length and design. Sentences should not be so complex that they interfere with understanding. Short sentences can help build excitement. And starting a sentence with "and," for instance, emphasizes that you have something more to say:

> It slices. It dices. It juliennes. And it comes with a one-year, money-back guarantee!

Complete your first draft. Before writing most documents, choose a title or a working title. For email, write a subject line. For ads, write a headline and, if appropriate, a subhead.

You might revise them after you complete your first draft, but get something down on paper or on your computer screen to anchor your work. Once you start your body copy, write swiftly from outline point to outline point.

Make sure spell check and grammar check are turned off. All they do is point out mistakes before it's time to edit. They disrupt your train of thought and interfere with creativity. If you are producing a long document, take a break after you complete each section or several sections.

Revision, Editing, Proofreading

Edit your documents before sending them out. Go back to your planning notes and ask yourself if you have captured the purpose of the document using language that appeals to your target market. If not, review your notes and edit. If so, proofread to correct any errors. If not, review your notes and edit.

With ad copy, you can break the rules of grammar. However, that does not mean you *should* break the rules of grammar. Break them consciously. When you revise, you can ensure that you have followed the rules of grammar or broken them for a particular effect. Break them too often in one copy block and you risk alienating your reader. And your copy will sound forced and insincere.

Print your document to proof it. You will be amazed at what the eye catches when working from the page as opposed to the computer screen. Read your work out loud as well. If it's awkward to read, it's awkwardly written.

Chapter 6: Target Market & Headlines

If you don't know whom you are talking to, how do you know what to write? This is so crucial, it's worth repeating:

> If you don't know whom you are talking to, how do you know what to write?

You have to know your audience or target market before you can perform (write) for that audience. If you were advertising your product in the *Toronto Star*, a newspaper read by several hundred thousand people every day, you would want your ad to leap off the page and attract as many readers as possible. Or would you? You want it to leap off the page and *attract members of your target market* who are reading the paper.

If I am not in your target market, the chances of me stopping at your ad for more than a second or two are slim to none. And if you make me stop, the chances of me buying are zero. So why try to target everybody?

If you are advertising a product with mass appeal on a TV show like *The Simpsons*, you have to be creative and inventive enough to prevent viewers from clicking the remote or leaving the room when your commercial comes on. But your ad's creative concept also has to separate your target market from the rest of the viewers. Seldom does a product, even a so-called mass-market one, appeal to *every* reader or viewer. Think of all the products that you see advertised and never, ever buy. You might even like some of the ads, but if you are not in the target market, you are not going to buy the advertised product.

If you are a wine drinker only, you are not going to buy beer—unless you are having a party and are buying all the alcohol for it. If you are a vegetarian, you are not going to buy meat. If you are an audiophile, you are not going to shop at Joe's Bargain Basement Electronics. And so it goes. Not everyone is in your target market. If you try to appeal to all, you will appeal to nobody.

When it comes to business-to-business advertising, companies are more inclined to advertise in trade magazines (publications dedicated to the interests of a specific trade or industry) or use direct mail. The trade magazine delivers the message directly to a group more likely to be the advertiser's target market. For instance, if you sell forms to legal firms, you will most likely advertise in a trade magazine read by lawyers or use direct mail sent to lawyers.

Just because you are using a medium that reaches your target market directly, your ad cannot be dull or boring. It is still competing for attention against all the other ads in the publication, as well as the articles. Just because you are mailing your message to law firms, it does not mean that the direct mail piece can be pedantic or uninspired. The recipient must still be motivated to open and read the direct mail piece, as detailed in various chapters in the book.

Let me give you an example of how important knowing your target market is, or of how not knowing whom you are writing for equates with not knowing what to write. My daughter, then 13, expressed frustration with an end-of-year school assignment that she should have loved: Write and act in a commercial that would entice tourists to Paris. My daughter loves theatre arts, but she was frustrated.

"We shouldn't be working at this time of year," she said.

"But you love this stuff!"

"But we have to do it in French and my accent sucks."

"You can work the camera or be a mime...."

"The whole thing is stupid," she shrugged. "Carol wants to be a model. She wants me to be a university student. Dylan wants to be a chef. Jessica wants to make a dance video. And we don't have anything to say...."

Immediately, I understood the problem. But I could not tell her. If you have a 13-year-old, you know they have to solve their own problems, even when it seems as if they are asking you for advice.

"Who is it you want to come to Paris?" I asked.

"Anybody. I don't know. Anybody who travels."

"Anybody?"

"I guess so."

"What if you were creating a commercial for romantic couples on their honeymoon? What would you say to them?"

"Ick! I don't know."

"That's fair. But would it be different than if you were talking to, say, gay couples?"

She rolled her eyes, but played along. "Sure, I guess."

"And what about wine lovers or people who love art?"

"A wine lover could love art."

"That's true."

"What about students?" she asked me.

I could see the wheels beginning to turn. "What about them?"

"Would they come to Paris?"

"Nah." I played devil's advocate. "They don't have money."

"But don't some students come to Paris to study? I remember reading about that."

"I think they do. But what does this have to do with your ad?"

"I have to call Carol," she said and disappeared.

A few minutes later, she was off to Carol's to write the commercial—the enthusiasm I know she has for theatre arts readily apparent.

In the final commercial, one that appeals directly to a well-defined target market, Carol is in modelling school, Kyah is an acting student (one who speaks; not a mime), Dylan is in chef's school and Jessica is a ballet student. They invite Canadian students to come spend a year studying in Paris. The Canucks will be able to study and learn French, stay in inexpensive university dorms, drink cheap wine, and have a great deal of fun with an instant community of other students.

Now you can claim that almost anyone with discretionary income is a potential tourist. However, a 30-second commercial or a one-page (or smaller) newspaper or magazine ad cannot be all things to all people—not if it's going to be targeted and effective.

I am sure, though, that you've seen such generic ads running in the travel section of your newspaper. Who reads the travel section? People who want to travel and are shopping for the best price to a particular destination. So those ads are not meant to entice readers to come to Paris (or other destinations) as much as they are meant to entice price-conscious travellers who are planning trips to Paris or other locations to select a particular airline or tour company. In that way, they are reaching their target market.

Before she knew her audience, Kyah thought she knew her product (tourist attractions, restaurants and art galleries). Once she found her audience, or target market, a whole other world of product features and benefits—low-cost accommodation, living with peers, partying, and studying abroad—became apparent.

Once she found her target market, she could focus her message on the features and benefits that appealed to that niche group and write her commercial for them—using language, characters and images that they could relate to. Writing became fun—something she wanted to do.

If you learn nothing else from this book, *learn that you have to know for whom you are writing.* You have to define your target market as specifically as possible. Only then do you define the impression or image you want the target market to associate with your product and the action you want them to take. You can also then begin to define the features and benefits of your product that appeal to that market.

Again, before you do anything, pinpoint your target market. Then write or produce an effective advertisement or commercial—one that speaks to your target market using concepts, situations, language and images to which they can relate.

Target Market Defined

Target Market. A segment of the market that is the strategic focus of a business or a marketing plan.

Normally the members of this segment possess common characteristics and a relatively high propensity to purchase a particular product or service. Because of this, the members of this segment represent the greatest potential for sales volume and frequency.

The target market is often defined in terms of geography (physical location), demographics (age, gender, sexual orientation, income bracket and/or education), and psychographics (psychological traits, characteristics or lifestyle). Your concept (and related image and headline) should resonate with the target market on an emotional and/or intellectual level. It should capture the attention of your target market and engage your audience. It should make your target market curious or otherwise aroused—emotionally, intellectually or sexually.

With that in mind, let's deconstruct several headlines to find out how they do what they do. (See Chapter 27: Appendix I for comments on each of the headlines, below.)

Headline:

Take a Walk on the Mild Side

- What product or service do you think this headline is promoting?
- From what has this headline been derived?
- Is there anything familiar about this headline?
- Does this headline engage you?
- How might it engage the target market?
- Who is the target market for this headline? Why?
- What is the target market's connection with the product or service promoted?
- What is the purpose of the ad?

Headline:

Over 40? Acne Blemishes?

- What product or service is this headline promoting?
- Who is the target market?
- How old is the target market?
- What condition does the target market have?
- How does this headline separate its target market from other readers?
- Why does it do so? Why so blunt?
- What is the purpose of the ad?

Headline:

They Laughed When I Sat Down
At The Piano
But When I Started To Play!

- What product or service is this headline promoting?
- Who is the target market? How old is the target market? Why?
- What does the target market desire (or need)?
- How does this headline promise to fulfill it?
- What is the purpose of the ad?

Headline:

If you are a non-drinker, you can save 20% on life insurance.

- What product or service is this headline promoting?
- Who is the target market? How old is the target market? Why?
- What does the target market desire?
- What conditions are required to qualify?
- How does that focus the ad?
- What is the purpose of the ad?

Headline:

APHROADISIAC

- What product or service is this headline promoting?
- Who is the target market? How old is the target market?
- How does this headline play on words?
- What desire does it create?
- What is the purpose of the ad?

Let's take a closer look at that last headline in context:

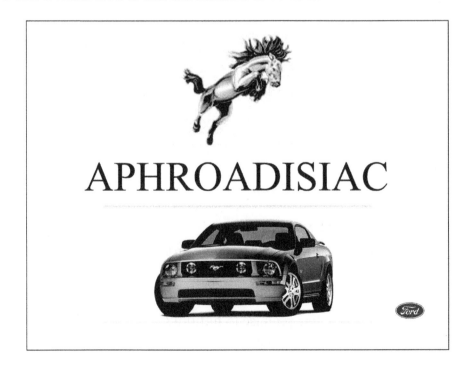

A solid, effective, well-targeted headline can paint a vivid picture, but context does make a difference. With the above visual in mind:

- What is the concept (or hook or theme) of this ad?
- What is the purpose of the ad?
- Who is the target market? How old is the target market? Why?
- How does this headline play on words?

> **Concept Connection**: Are you starting to get the connection between the product, the target market and the purpose of the ad? Do you see why the purpose of some ads is something *other* than to sell?

Do ads that build brand awareness or position products facilitate sales? If they do not, the advertising industry is wasting billions of dollars each year. (Some may argue that the ad industry wastes billions each year, regardless.) And if ads only facilitate, but do not close, sales, then that poses the question: What does the advertiser have to do to actually get somebody to buy something?

All good questions. They will be addressed as we progress.

Chapter 7: The Tip of the Iceberg

Copywriting is the tip of the iceberg. There is much you need to know—the base of the 'berg, so to speak—before you begin to write. Sometimes, clients don't know this. They think they can hand you a product and tell you to write. They expect you to produce polished copy without asking any questions. But how can you write if you don't know the purpose of the ad, the needs/desires of the target market, the product features and benefits, and so on?

Pretend I am one of those in-a-hurry clients. I have apples. You are a copywriter. "Here," I say. "Produce an ad about my apples!" What do you need to know before you begin to write? Make a list.

- *Before I begin to write the copy, I need to know:*

Use a separate sheet of paper and list everything you think you need to know before you start to write.

After all I've written I'm going to presume you have a target market and purpose on your list. If not, add them to you list! Once you've created your full list, turn to Chapter 27 and compare your list to the list in Appendix II to see many of the things you would want to consider before writing an ad about apples.

More Lists and Writing Exercises

Create a similar list for *honey*. What do you need to know before you can even begin to think of writing copy about honey? Jot it all down on a list. Don't forget to include your target market (define it as best you can) and purpose on your list.

Once you have created your lists for apple and honey, cluster either word and freefall for five minutes. See where that takes you....

Once you have completed your clustering and your freefall, find a hook or concept, one that will appeal to your defined target market. Don't fret if you feel stymied. We'll do more work on this later, but I want to see what you can come up with as a kind of gut instinct. After all, you have to hang your headline, subhead and body copy on an idea of some kind, and that idea should relate in some way to your product and appeal to or attract the attention of your target market.

Once you have your hook, take some time to write several potential headlines and subheads that reflect it.

Once you have several headlines and subheads, write a block of body copy for honey or for apple. This doesn't have to be stellar copy and you don't have to hit every point on your list. Give it a shot and produce what you might consider a rough first draft of an ad that hits the major points you feel you need to address to speak to your defined target market and achieve your purpose.

Not Done Yet

Now I want you to try something similar for a computer (you can choose from a Windows-based PC or a Mac, from a desktop to a laptop) or a cell phone (such as a RIM Blackberry, an Apple iPhone, or any other so-called smart-phone brand you are aware of).

You don't have to make a comprehensive list. Try to think of at least five points you'd address in your ad. Then define your target market and your purpose—do you want to sell, create brand awareness, demonstrate your ability to solve a problem, associate your product with something your target market desires, a combination of some of those? And so on.

Create a concept based on the product, target market and purpose. Once you've done that, write a headline and subhead. If it helps, and it should help, cluster the product name and write a short freefall before you come up with your concept and writer your headline.

Once you have your concept, headline and subhead, stop there.

Next step: Take a moment and review your concept, headline and subhead and ask yourself this: *Am I targeting a consumer or a business audience?*

With your answer in mind, flip your target market. If you were targeting a consumer audience, I want you to target a business audience. You can choose if you want to target a small business or large enterprise. If you were targeting a business audience, target a consumer audience instead.

Go through the above creative process again and produce a new headline and subhead. Be conscious of how changing your target market shapes and influences the points you'd address, your purpose, your concept, and your actual writing—the writing of your headline and subhead.

✎ ✎ ✎

As Your Audience Changes...

I think you get the picture, but allow me to summarize. As your audience (target market) changes, so too does your message—the points you want to address, the image you want to portray, your purpose, your concept, and your writing—the headline, subhead and body copy.

For the computer or phone, in the case of a consumer audience, you might want someone to walk into a retail outlet and buy your product. But if they are not aware of your product, or if they think another product in the same category is more effective, less expensive or sexier, you might have to do some educating first. It all depends on how you compete against similar products in the category.

For a small-business audience, you might want an owner or office manager to walk into a retail outlet and buy your product; but you also might want someone from the company to pick up the phone and ask for a sales representative to visit, or you might want someone from the company to include you in a request for proposal (RFP). That, too, is what you might want the purchasing manager from a larger enterprise to do. In this case, however, you might want the director of information technology (IT) to call and talk to your sales representative about a demonstration of your product(s), and to discuss your products and service agreements before putting together the RFP.

If you think that makes sense for computer products or cell phones, but not for apples or honey, ask yourself how your copy for apples or honey would change for the following:

- consumer audience, middle-class families of four
- consumer audience, health-conscious joggers
- consumer audience, health-conscious consumers who eat only locally grown organic food
- local green grocers
- national grocery store chains
- small local bakeries
- industrial packaged food producers

As your audience changes, so does a lot of the pre-writing thinking you do, as does the actual copy you write.

Beyond the writing, or words, your ad (brochure, web page, and so on) most likely will include typestyles (fonts) of various sizes, graphics, pictures and/or other images, and other elements—all of which we will take a quick look at.

The Elements of an Ad

The ad below incorporates the basic elements of a print advertisement in the classic layout style:

- *Image* on top
- *Headline* and *subhead* beneath the image
- *Body copy* in a block below the headline
- *Call to action*, in this instance a modest one, at the end of the ad
- *Logo* and *slogan* used to visually anchor the ad, literally helping to draw the reader's eye from the image through to the end of the ad

---

Call to Action: A marketing and sales device that tells the customer how to take the next step towards a purchase or execute an activity. Often accompanied by a time-limited incentive to act.

Combined, all the elements form a graphic image. While the words you use in your ad must support a hook or concept that appeals to your target market, the entire ad must project a predetermined product or corporate image that also appeals to your target market. That image helps position your brand, product and/or company. In short, all the components of your ad—layout, graphics/photo, headline, subhead, body copy, logo, slogan and call to action—must appeal to the target market and serve your ad's purpose.

It's the copywriter's job to focus on the copy, or what I call the tip of the iceberg. However, there are times when you get to comment on the layout, graphics, typestyle and other components. If you know the target market, the purpose of the ad, and how the company wants to be perceived (all part of the iceberg's base), you will be in a better position to make big picture comments about the look and feel of the ad.

This is a book about copywriting, not graphic design, but do look at the *faux* ad below. Once you have looked at it and read it, move on to the next chapter where the base of the iceberg will be revealed.

It's a Jungle out there

Advertising that roars loudly is noticed.

What a jungle. So many ads. All on the prowl for attention.

If you want to pounce on readers.... If you want them to notice your ads.... If you want them to remember your ad.... You have to roar. **Loudly**. Louder than the other animals in the advertising jungle.

However, ads that make a memorable *roar* are not easy to create. All the ad elements—concept, design, photos, illustrations and copy—must work together to capture the attention of your target market.

How do you do that? Aim for the heart. Or the head. Or both. With bold concepts that your target market can relate to. With meaningful images that mesmerize the reader. With powerful and strategic words that hit the mark.

Bellow like Tarzan. When Tarzan bellowed, jungle animals moved into action. Your ad should have a *call to action*. It might be LOUD. It could be a whisper. A *buy now* hard sell. Or something as simple as your company's contact information.

Whatever it is, it should be there. So the reader knows what to do next. And how to do it.

Elephant Advertising

416-xxx-xxxx | www.elphantsneverforget.com

Unforgettable Advertising

Chapter 8: The Base of the Iceberg

If copywriting is the tip of the iceberg, then the marketing strategy is its base. Once the marketing strategy is revealed, or you convince the client to reveal it (this can be like pulling teeth), you engage in creative brainstorming exercises to move from the base to the point where you are ready to write—to find your concept and some of the words and phrases that you will use in your copy.

In print advertising, you generally write your copy to fit an ad layout. The layout, as we have seen, indicates where the headline, subhead, body copy and slogan go, all in relation to any images or illustrations. The layout also indicates the type size of the copy. Given a defined space in a layout and type size, you can calculate how many words you need. Suddenly all that creative energy must fit into a headline of maybe five to seven words and a copy box of 25 or 50 words.

Remember: Writing is a process. Do not write to fit the copy block, initially. Write long. Then edit for focus, and then for fit. You do this for several reasons. First off, you do not want space or word count to inhibit creativity. Secondly, as any writer will tell you, it is easier to cut copy to make words fit a space than it is to pad or expand copy to make words fit the space. Occasionally, the copy is written first, and the ad is designed around the words. However, generally speaking, the layout (reflecting the concept or hook) is produced first.

For broadcast, you write your copy to fit an allotted amount of time—usually 30 or 60 seconds. Again, the concept or hook is developed first. And just because you have 30 or 60 seconds to fill, it does not mean you write to fill 30 or 60 seconds. Other audio elements—introductory music, sound effects, and a jingle—might fill some of the commercial time. Also, silence can be golden when used effectively in a broadcast commercial. In so many ways, what you write—the space or the time you fill and how you fill it—all depends on the concept.

In short, in print advertising and broadcast commercials, all the elements come together as part of the creative process—although the creative process often includes negotiations between the creative director, graphic artist or commercial director, writer and, oh, the client, the person who is spending the money and gets the final say.

While it might seem like the concept is the base of the iceberg, that is not the case. It is the foundation of your copy. The marketing strategy is the base of the iceberg. As you will see, it contains far more information than you can squeeze into an ad, but it is difficult to develop an effective concept and write an ad without the marketing strategy.

You do not begin to write until you have a marketing strategy, or road map, to get you from where you are to where you want to be. Marketing strategies, part of the overall marketing plan, vary in length; some companies do not produce formal plans. However, whether they are written down (highly recommended) or contained in the head of business owners or marketing executives, most marketing strategies follow seven stages.

Seven-Stage Marketing Strategy:

Here is the basic seven-stage marketing program you should go through before you start writing:

- **Stage 1**: Define your product or service
- **Stage 2**: Choose your target market
- **Stage 3**: Know your competition and USP
  - o USP: Unique Sale Proposition, or that which differentiates you from the competition
- **Stage 4: Understand advertising's business environment**
  - o Economic, Political, Legal, Social/Cultural, Technological
- **Stage 5**: Produce a promotional strategy objective
- **Stage 6**: Create your sales message
- **Stage 7**: Select promotional media

There are additional stages, such as setting promotional and production budgets and conducting your media buy. However, these go beyond the scope of this book. Suffice it to say that someone has to buy the broadcast time or print space, or ads would never make it to air or into print. And all ads or ad campaigns have budgets—productions budgets, or the cost of producing the ad or commercial, plus media buy budgets.

With those budget caveats in mind, writers should not begin writing until they understand the seven-stage marketing strategy. The strategy is usually presented to the creative team (creative director, art director, senior copywriter and account manager) by the client or their marketing representative. (Some large ad agencies will help clients develop their marketing strategies.) However, sometimes a business owner tells a copywriter and graphic artist what he or she wants to achieve and says, "Do it for me."

Below is the seven-stage marketing strategy for a fictional soft drink or pop that we are calling *Very Cherry Vanilla Cola*, or VCVC or VC^2.

Marketing Strategy: Very Cherry Vanilla Cola (VCVC; VC^2)

What you see here is a trimmed-down version of the full marketing strategy for our fictional soft drink.

An actual marketing strategy can go on for dozens and dozens of pages. Of course, such detailed strategies would include all the research information that supports the claims we are about to fabricate in the VCVC marketing strategy. Still, this is more than you may get from some clients.

Stage 1: Define your product or service

Describe the attributes of your product in terms of features and benefits:

- **Features**: Cola base, vanilla kick, cherry sweet, dash of caffeine; off-brand price.
- **Benefits**: Familiar, yet different in taste; real kick; affordable; scoring exceptionally well in blind taste-test comparisons.
- **Positioning** The Party Pop (for those who can't drink, or choose not to drink, alcohol).

Stage 2: Choose your target market

- **Age**: 16 to 24; primarily first-year college and university; will spill over into older and younger groups.
- **Gender**: Primarily male (seen as early adopters and influencers).
- **Income**: From mid- to upper-income families; they have allowance or part-time jobs and want to spend their money on entertainment and clothes; we quench their thirst and give them a kick for less.
- **Other Factors**: Urban kids with a funky attitude, involved in sports like skateboarding, snowboarding; into rap and hip-hop, electronic stuff; younger kids look up to them.

Stage 3: Know your competition and USP

- Coke, Pepsi, Mountain Dew and blended-flavour pops targeted at a younger demographic.
- **USP** (what we have that the competition does not): More kick, unique combination of tastes and lower price.
- The competition is familiar but they are the tired and stale status quo.

- VCVC currently has no brand awareness; it will be available primarily in mom-and-pop and chain convenience stores in urban centres, and vending machines in/near schools and recreation centres.

Stage 4: Understand advertising's business environment

- **Economic**: Teens and young adults have limited budgets; VCVC delivers more *kick* for less.

- **Political**: Difficult to get into some schools due to sugar/caffeine issues, or that sell exclusive vending machine space to one company; will have distribution implications.

- **Legal**: There are those who want to restrict the use of caffeine in pop; we meet legal limits but we don't want to overplay *kick* and get opponents of caffeine in cola in a lather. It is part of our USP, so we can't ignore it. Let word of mouth work in our favour?

- **Social/Cultural**: The move to healthier eating may work in our favour. It's aimed at boomers (once the counterculture). We are positioning VCVC as the new counter culture pop—the pop your parents will not drink. Also, there is a move away from alcohol on university campuses, especially at frosh parties, initiations and sanctioned events—VCVC can fill that gap.

- **Technological**. Target market is into the web, online chat, cell phones and other current technology. VCVC will launch a website with chat rooms, develop cell-phone ring tones and pop-culture news alerts.

Stage 5: Promotional Strategy Objective

- **Fulfillment**: Maslow's need is *thirst*, but target market does not need VCVC. They can drink water! So the ad should play on a *personal desire* and *associate* drinking VCVC with fulfillment of that desire.

- **Target Market's desire**: To be perceived as cool, above the fray. Desires friends and fun. Wants to be seen as counterculture, intelligent, active—but not with Mom and Dad. Peers and image with peers are important.

- **Brand Awareness**. Target market is not aware of brand, but they drink pop. Make them aware and persuade potential early adopters to switch.

- **Phase 1 of Ad Campaign:** Create *Brand Awareness* and *Position* VCVC as a party pop; let pricing be surprise/bonus. Motivate target market to switch to VCVC. Requires memorable, in-your-face concept.
  - **Phase 1 Promotional Strategy Objective:** Within three months, make 50% of target market in Toronto and Vancouver (test markets) aware of VCVC; have 15% try it without inducement.

- **Note:** So you can see what comes next, we will include the following:
Phase 2 of the Ad Campaign: Once brand awareness is established and early adopters have tried VCVC, we will launch *it-costs-less* ads and use discount coupons to spark mass sales.

Stage 6: Write your sales message

- Inform target market that they can *get unique taste and a sweet kick for less with the new party pop.*
- **Slogan**: Convey sales message in creative manner, like Nike's "Just Do It" or McDonald's "I'm lovin' it!"

Stage 7: Select Promotional Media

- Media must reach defined target market and allow us to accomplish our promotional strategy.
- Full-page ads in selected college and university newspapers and in magazines read by target market.
- No TV, radio or transit ads *initially.* Creative will influence future transit ads and the VCVC website (which will have cool contests, games, entertainment news, chat rooms, and so on).
- Posters in university washrooms can replicate full-page ads.
- **Deliverable:** Concept and related image/graphic ideas; headline, subhead, body copy, slogan.

Questions for the Client

Once the marketing plan is presented, the creative team gets to ask the client questions, such as:

- What colour, size and shape is the bottle (or can)?
- What colour is the pop?
- Does it have a particular odour?
- Is the product sold individually or in six- and 12-packs?

The client's presentation would include all that information. However, for the sake of any writing you attempt, you can make up the answers to these questions. Whatever your answers, they should appeal to your target market.

Once the client has answered your questions, you go away and drink many martinis (all billed back to the client) and then come up with a concept (or concepts) and proposed images and headlines—plus your rationale for them. You present the concepts (you might demonstrate them in a rough layout) to the client who approves one (you hope). Then you finalize the layout and copy outline (the copy points that your ad will include).

Once that is approved, you write your ad. Sometimes, the client will select two or three concepts from the dozen you present, and then you can produce layouts and copy points or final copy for each of them before the client makes a final selection.

Moving From Base to Tip of the Iceberg

So how do you come up with the concept? Where do you begin? Remember the creative exercises presented in Chapter 4? Now we put them into action. Before starting, go back to Chapter 4 and refresh your memory. Then read the pre-copywriting exercises, listed below. They are meant to help you brainstorm and develop concepts or hooks on which you can hang your copy.

Here is how you give yourself a whack on the creative side on the brain:

You don't have to do all of these exercises, but I'd suggest you do at least five. Try not to think too much about what you are doing. Just do them with an open mind and see what comes up. Later, you will turn some of your brainstorming into copy.

So here's what you do:

1. **Cluster**: VCVC, then flip into....

2. **Freefall** (5 minutes)

3. **Directed Freefall**: *A day without VCVC is like a day without....* (3 minutes)

4. **Directed Freefall** (complete each in short bursts): VCVC tastes like.... feels like.... smells like.... sounds like.... looks like....

5. **Become target market and answer the following:**
   - Favourite sport (on TV)?
   - Favourite sport (participates)?
   - Favourite movie or actor/actress?
   - Favourite band/singer/song?
   - Favourite food?
   - Grossed out when.... Ticked off when.... Loves it when....
   - Favourite saying or expression?
   - First impression you make on opposite sex?
   - Lasting impression you leave?
   - You like the kind of (girl/guy) who....

6. **Testimonial**: Become target market (in your mind) and freefall complete this line: "I drink VCVC because...."

7. **Testimonial**: Become anti-target market and freefall complete this line: "You *shouldn't* drink VCVC because...."

8. **Complete the following**: "To get my hands on VCVC, I'd...." (Freefall for a couple of minutes)

9. **Confined Spaces**: Put target market members into a confined space—elevator, wrestling ring, rocket to Mars, or whatever, and freefall a conversation between them....

10. **Before & After**: What was the person representing your target market thinking/doing/feeling just before thinking of or buying VCVC? What was that person thinking/doing/feeling right after taking the first sip of VCVC?

11. **Animal:** Pick an animal that represents VCVC:
    - Why that animal?
    - List its personality/physical traits/emotional attributes
    - Let the animal speak (freefall)....

12. **Lists:**
    - Reasons one should not drink pop; reasons one should....
    - Who drinks VCVC; who does not....
    - What VCVC drinkers do; what they do not....
    - Other lists that you can think of....

13. **Martian anthropologist**: You have never tasted pop. You land on earth, open the door of your spaceship, meet a dude (or dudette) who twists the top off a bottle of VCVC and hands it to you. You chug-a-lug and....
    - Shout one word/phrase....
    - Followed by ... a short freefall....

✐ ✐ ✐

Find the Hook, and....

Now that you have done all that creative work, find the hook and hang your copy on it. Is it really that easy? For some of you, perhaps. Others might have to go mining. Go through all you have written and see if you can find some creative gold. But what are you looking for? Let's break it down logically.

You are looking for a great idea. You might find it in a great line of copy. The line might inspire a related image. You might find the idea somewhere in your brainstorming. In might inspire a line of copy and image that isn't in your brainstorming, but you might find the idea, line of copy and image in your brainstorming.

What makes them great? They seem to jump out at you (or at your target market, actually). They speak to and capture the attention of your target market. The great idea (the headline and image that form your concept), say, shout, something like:

> Hey! Stop! Just for a second. And feel engaged, at some level, because VCVC is associated with whatever it is that engages you.

So go mining through your brainstorming material and look for your hook or concept. In other words, write out your *hook* on which you can hang your headline and an image. It could be a few words or phrases, or a sentence.

Then What do You do?

Your concept should be clear in your mind, even if the words that make up your hook are not as pithy as possible. Now you turn your hook into the following:

- Headline (approximately one to seven words)
- Subhead (approximately three to 10 words)
- An image tied into your headline and/or subhead

Then write a short block of copy, your body copy. Make sure you build on your hook in your body copy by using words and phrases that relate to your hook (the poetry of your copy). Write the following:

- Body copy (approximately 25 to 75 words; don't worry about overwriting because you can edit to fit); see Pre-writing of Body Copy below.
- Use short, incomplete sentences. Why? Because. You can.
- Or don't use them. Use whatever feels right for your target market and your concept and purpose.

And finally, to end the ad, write this:

- Slogan (one to seven words). It does not have to reflect your hook, although it can. Consider it a final thought about your product; your final word to your target audience.

Body Copy Pre-writing

If it helps, before writing your body copy, jot down several copy points you feel your ad should hit. The points, for the most part, should relate to your concept. There may be some points you want to make about the product that are not connected to the concept—price, location where the product is available, guaranties, and so on. They are there if need be to help you achieve your purpose.

Arrange your copy points in order of importance. This is your outline. Once you have your outline points arranged, write your rough first draft. Swing from vine to vine (outline point to outline point) or freefall from point to point.

If you feel like you have completed your first draft but have not hit all your copy points, relax. Maybe you don't need to hit them all. You can look at that when you edit, when you take a logical, linear, left-brain look at what you have written. If you are missing something, work it in. If you have too much copy and have hit too many points, to the stage where your ad has lost its focus, cut copy. Make your copy as powerful and as focused as possible.

When writing, keep in mind the following: Your goal for this particular ad is to create *brand awareness*—to associate this product with something that your target market relates to. So you will most likely not use a great deal of copy. You might even avoid, for this particular ad, the mundane—such as price, location, guaranties, and so on.

On the Other Hand...

Because the creative process works differently for all of us, feel free to ignore what I've said. If none of the above feels right, break the boundaries and do your own thing! Just make sure you are capturing the attention of the defined target market and writing copy that helps you achieve your purpose.

If You Are Having Difficulty...

All of that is easy for me to say. You may have some great concepts (yes, concepts—plural!) and boffo copy. You may have some great concepts and not know it. You may still feel blank. If so, let me help you tie your creative work with the logical process, described above.

First of all, you really have to let loose when doing the brainstorming. Nothing is too absurd. And if it feels like it is, don't censor yourself. That you can do later, when you go mining for gold. If you find something, as you scour your lists, clusters and freefalls, that seems way out there, pull it back and see if it works. Or push it further out there. You are launching this new product, so you want to be noticed!

At some point, the penny will drop and you will experience that "aha!" moment. You will find words, phrases, images that you can use to define your concept or hook. And then you look for related words—the words that you use to build on your theme.

Or, you might find a hook and realize that nothing else in your brainstorming connects to it. Fine. Cluster your hook, try some freefalls, and see where that takes you. Again, your hook might be an image. If so, just add words. It might be a word or phrase. If so, conjure up the associated image.

The key is to find that hook—word, phrase, image or idea—that you can hang your copy on. Once you have your hook or concept (or several potential hooks), create a headline and subhead that relate to your concept and image. Then write your body copy.

When reviewing your first draft, look for the most powerful words, phrases or lines. If they are not in your headline, question your headline. You might save them for the end—a punch-line, so to speak. At this point, *it all depends.*

It all depends on what? The only thing that can guide you is your subjective gut reaction. However, keep your target market in mind. You have to capture attention first, or the ad will flop.

Remember your purpose. Make sure your copy—headline, subhead and image in particular—connect to your concept. Ensure also that a theme—established by the concept, image and headline—flows through your body copy.

End with a slogan. No simple task, that. Some companies pay tens or hundreds of thousands of dollars to develop a slogan. I am asking you to simply jot one down. However, look at all the work you've done. It's probably there in your creative work—a million-dollar slogan!

Let your work sit for a day to obtain some distance from it so that you can see the forest for the trees, so to speak. Revise it, keeping in mind the marketing plan, target market, purpose ... and ... you are done.

But is it Effective Copy?

This is where you have to test it. Bounce if off others, including representatives of your target market. Revise it as may be required before showing it to your client for approval. Be prepared to revise again. Or, start all over again if the concept doesn't fly.

Note: If you are using this book as part of a course, then there should be opportunity to bounce your copy off classmates and the instructor. If you are not using this book as part of a course, I encourage you to try the exercises with an open mind and come up with at least three concepts. Perhaps you can bounce your work off friends and colleagues. Once you finish reading this book, review the case studies in Chapter 26 and apply the creative process to them as well.

Chapter 9: Headlines and Copy Blocks

From the copywriter's perspective, the headline is key to the ad. That is where you shine. It is where you tie the words to the concept (and ad image). It is where your words, in conjunction with the image, *capture the attention* of the reader. And you only have mere seconds to capture the interest of your audience with your headline.

A headline makes 80% of the impact of an ad—as long as the graphics have captured the reader's attention, and the headline is speaking to your target market.

<u>Five times</u> as many people read the headlines as read the body copy. If the image and headline don't capture attention, the reader will move on. That is why the headline *must* use words that appeal in some way to the target market. In other words, if your headline appeals to the wrong audience, you are wasting your client's money.

Below are some examples of headlines that have been successful in the past. Do any of them pique your interest or curiosity? Why? Why not? Try to determine whom the headlines are appealing to (and how they are doing this) and what products or services they are promoting.

- How a fool stunt made me a star salesman!
- Be the next one on your block to own a Radio Shack TRS-80
- Is your computer system prepared for the year 2000?
- How I retired at age 40—with a guaranteed income for life!
- How to lose 30 pounds in 30 days.
- Does she ... or doesn't she?
- Look Ma, no cavities!
- Are you ever tongue-tied at a party?
- Hands that look lovelier in 24 hours, or your money back
- Guaranteed to go through ice, mud or snow, or we pay the tow.
- Pierced by 301 nails… retains full pressure
- Is the life of a child worth $1 to you?
- To people who want to write, but can't get started

- Who else wants a lighter cake, in half the mixing time?
- When doctors "feel rotten" this is what they do

Test Headlines

The market response to headlines should be tested. The purpose of testing is to demand maximum performance from every marketing effort. The only way to know what the marketplace thinks is by quantitatively measuring the results of your marketing.

Testing can be done by obtaining feedback from focus groups. If you are about to launch a national campaign, it can also be done in the field—by publishing an ad with two different headlines and two different response methods (such as two different post office boxes, telephone numbers, e-mail addresses or websites) to measure the differences in response. Once you know which headline was more successful, you can launch your national campaign.

Let's Become Headline Testers

Which headline do you think was more successful?

A. What would happen to her if something happened to you?

B. Your Retirement Income Plan

Headline A's response was 500% better than headline B. Overall, the ad was five times as successful.

Try these two:

A. How to turn your careful driving into money

B. Auto insurance at lower rates if you're a careful driver

Headline A had 1,200%, or 12 times, the response of Headline B, which looked appealing enough on the surface. You have to test since your personal preference or your guess as to how the market would respond could be wrong.

Think of headlines as your calling cards, inviting your audience to read. Since you only have seconds to capture the attention of your audience, headlines often play on words, fracture clichés, reflect song lyrics, challenge the reader, use innuendo or offer a benefit that excites the target market.

Loaded, high-impact, controversial or familiar lines are used as attention-grabbing devices—as a means of cutting through the clutter or noise, of all the competing ads out there. To be effective, they also have capture attention and speak to the target market.

Typefaces/Typestyles

What about the look of the headline—the typeface and typestyle? That is generally left up to the art director or designer, but there are a few things you should know about type.

There are two basic families of type: Serif and sans serif. Serif is considered the friendlier, warmer type; sans serif is considered the cleaner, easier-to-read type, especially when used in reverse:

> This is a sample of Serif type used in reverse.
> And of Sans Serif type used in reverse.

Within the two families, there are literally thousands of typestyles or typefaces, known as fonts. Type sizes range from:

8 point or smaller to

36 point and

larger

And there are variations within the typestyles, such as:

- **Serif and Sans Serif BOLD** and *Serif and Sans Serif Italics*

Generally, it is not a good idea to mix and match typestyles from different families because it makes copy (text) difficult to read, much to the detriment of your promotional piece. However, it is not uncommon to use a serif headline and sans serif body copy or vice versa.

Multiple Typeface Personalities

The creative director or ad designer usually selects the typeface, but the copywriter may be asked for input. Typefaces have personality. So when commenting on, or selecting, a typeface, keep in mind the personality of your target market, and the purpose of your ad.

When would you use the following typeface? For which type of products or services? For ads that run in which type of magazines? To appeal to which market segment? To achieve what purpose? Why?

Times New Roman	*Lucinda*
Arial	*Handwriting*
Comic	*Edwardian Script*
Impact	MATISSE
Broadway	**Rockwell**
CASTELLAR	Century Gothic
Square721	**croobie**

Body Copy

Headlines are all fine and well, but what about the body copy?

Writing is a craft. However, effective advertising can be elevated to an art. If you are sceptical, look at what Andy Warhol did with Campbell's Soup cans. He simply recreated a product container and called his paintings art. In addition to these now museum-pieces, real ads hang in the Smithsonian Museum. In the end, it's all subjective. But if you look closely at ad copy that works, you'll find a number of basic principles supporting the copy.

Get to know them. Apply them to your target market and the purpose of your ad.

20 Tips to Help You Write Great Copy

In today's competitive marketplace, it is difficult to have your copy stand out from the rest. To make your writing as effective as possible, take time to understand with whom you have to communicate and what you have to say, and then develop copy that communicates your message to your audience.

Writing effective copy will help you position your product or business, communicate with your target market, and fulfill the purpose of your ad.

The 20 copy tips below will help you formulate a winning strategy for writing and delivering great copy. However, do not follow them blindly, as copywriting is subjective.

In short, use the tips that are most appropriate to what you are trying to accomplish! And never forget your target market.

20 Copy Tips

Tip #1: Demonstrate Knowledge. Do your research and demonstrate that you know your business/product, your target market and/or its business, industry trends and so on. Do not excessively tout your greatness (see tip #4).

Tip #2: Use Short Sentences. They make it easier to grasp the message. Also, use bullet points or subheadings to create an easy way for the reader to scan your major concepts. Use small simple words; however, do not condescend.

Tip #3: Don't Overwhelm. Use language the target market understands. Do not use buzzwords. A full page of text does not (necessarily) make for a better ad. It may dilute the message.

Tip #4: Run From Pompous Words. If you have to explain a word, do not use it. For example, replace "promulgate" with "announce"; "incipient" with "beginning"; and "auspicious" with "favourable."

Tip #5: Educate—Don't Sell. Hard sell *can* be a turnoff. (There are times, though, when it is exactly what you require.) Address the target market's needs. Do not make business promises you cannot keep. Honesty builds credibility.

Tip #6: Use a Great Headline. Grab attention quickly. Do not make it long or complicated. Write from the target market's perspective. For instance, pose a question that prompts the reader to answer the way you intend. Make sure your headline is in harmony with the images and that the target market relates to both.

Tip #7: Strike a Nerve. Hit an emotion. Embrace the benefits. Build the buy-in. Connect with the target market. Relating to the reader by connecting to an emotion is effective.

Tip #8: Know Your Audience. Focus on the target market and understand what drives your audience. Know their business or know them as consumers. What do they need, want and/or desire? Should your ad appeal to need, desire, want?

Tip #9: Focus on Benefits. Do not just push features. Be sure to know and write about the most important benefits. Imagine your target marketing asking: "What is in it for me?" Answer that question!

Tip #10: Magnetize. Draw customers to you. Set yourself apart from the competition. Let the energy come through in your copy to convey your unique selling proposition (USP). It is critical that you place your copy in media that reaches your target market.

Tip #11: Make an Impact. Do not use words that need further explanation. Keep it brief. "We deliver quality service...." You will need to follow up with an explanation of "quality service." Is there a way to state this fact without requiring further explanation?

Tip #12: Be Client-centred. Do not write for yourself. Use the word "you" throughout your copy, rather than the word "we."

Tip #13: Show Your Image. How do you want to be perceived? Like Apple, IBM, Home Depot, or a Dollar Store? Make sure your copy and visuals reflect your desired image.

Tip #14: Bring out Your Personality. Give your target market a feel for your company's personality. That means you must first define a personality for your company (or the product you are selling).

Tip #15: Know how the Message Translates. If your copy is being used internationally, make sure your message gets through to everyone. See Chapter 25 for translation errors that should never have happened.

Tip #16: Be Organized. Don't jump between thoughts. Organize (outline) your thoughts when writing copy for an article, press release, or any other medium.

Tip #17: Be Consistent. Show consistency in the tone and style of your copy, typestyle, graphics and images in your ads, on your website and in collateral material (packaging, point of sale, business cards). Place all your materials out on a table. Do you see consistency?

Tip #18: Proofread. Read the copy backwards. Start at the end and read each word, working from right to left in the sentence. If you focus on the individual word, you are more likely to find typos.

Tip #19: Test Your Copy. Solicit feedback on the copy you are planning to use from a sample of your target market. This can prove to be valuable in creating the final copy.

Tip #20: Edit, Edit, Edit. Get feedback and edit accordingly. Get the message perfect. Read it, set it aside and read it again! Then have someone else read it. Get feedback and edit again.

Copy Blocks

As you may have noticed when looking at ads in this book or ads in general, the lines in copy blocks are not very long. They do not go from margin to margin; they tend to have a fair bit of white space around them.

Copy lines that run 25 to 50 characters (letters, spaces, numbers, and any other keyboard character such as %#@$) are easier to read than longer copy lines – especially those that run 60 or more characters in length or run from margin to margin with little white space.

When writing copy, use wider margins and boost your type size. This helps you keep your sentences, and your ideas, short. Write in short paragraphs as well. The line-breaks contribute to white space. That makes your work easier to read or scan. Like it or not, your readers will be more inclined to scan than read. So work with them, not against them.

If the layout has been produced, you can work with the art director or layout artist to calculate the character count for the headline, subhead and copy block. Copywriting may feel like a lonely endeavour, but it is a team sport. For instance, the art director may want you to write your headlines in a particular font. Some graphic artists write a fake headline in the font they want to use for the ad. That enables you to write a headline that fills the allocated space.

Nine Keys to Writing Effective Copy

Here are nine keys to keep in mind as you are writing. You do not apply all keys to all copy blocks. However, you should review them and make a conscious decision as to what you will use and what you will leave out.

You make this decision based on the seven-stage marketing plan, paying particular attention to your target market, the purpose of the ad, the product and the media the ad will appear in.

Why the media? Media influences the message in terms of space or time restrictions. Obviously, you can say more in a three-fold brochure than you can in a banner ad on the Web. You can demonstrate more in a TV commercial than you can on radio or in print.

Key # 1: Start with the prospect (target market) in mind. While it is important to know what you are writing about, don't try to write your final copy until you know whom you are writing for.

Key # 2: Gain attention. Use a headline that teases or one that promotes benefits. If you can pique curiosity, the prospect will have to read the subhead or body copy to get the punch-line. If you promise a benefit, the prospect will have to read to discover how to obtain it—how to solve a problem. Sometimes you can combine the two in a one-two punch:

> **Headline**: The End of the Stone Age
>
> **Subhead**: Get rid of kidney stones—without surgery!

Key # 3: Make your ad FABulous: Features. **A**ssets. **B**enefits. You do not need to detail every FAB. In fact, if you emphasize everything, you emphasize nothing! However, the reader must know the primary features (what a product is or has), assets (what a product does and its advantages over the competition), and benefits (what's in it for the person thinking about buying the product). FAB changes with respect to your target market and the purpose of the ad.

For a price-conscious consumer who is shopping around:

> **Feature Headline**:
> The Panasonic 53" Wide-screen TV
>
> **Asset Subhead**:
> Brilliant viewing at the low price of $2,999
>
> **Benefit Subhead**:
> A $500 savings! See more—for less!

If the ad were running in a magazine that appealed to wealthy, high-end home theatre enthusiasts, how would the copy be different? What FAB aspects would you emphasize?

Key # 4: Differentiate from the competition. Take two oranges. They are both round and orange. But what if one were grown on a large commercial farm in Florida and the other on a small organic farm in California? What effect would that have on your copy? Which advantages would you stress for the organic orange? Which might you avoid? Where would you run the ad for it? Are there any advantages to the commercial orange? Or is it more like commercial beer— many brands that all pretty much taste the same? If so, how could you *position* the commercial orange? How could you create *brand awareness*?

Key # 5: Be the 3 C's: Clear, Compelling and Conversational. Adapt the tone of the ad to the publication. Ads in supermarket tabloids take on a decidedly different tone than those in the *Wall Street Journal*. If your ad is running in a business publication, be business-like. Or play against type and fracture the business-like expectations of the reader.

Key # 6: Overcome objections, suspicion and doubt. Always tell the truth. Always prove claims. Always reverse the risk by using trial offers, warranties and money-back guarantees. The more complex and expensive the product, the more important it is to overcome objections, suspicion and doubt. But keep the ad's purpose in mind. If you are positioning the product, then the concept is critical. If you are trying to close the sale (see Chapter 15: Direct Response Marketing), then overcoming objections, suspicion and doubt is of paramount importance. But you still have to get your prospect to read! See Key #2.

Key # 7: Write for readers, but format or design for scanners. You have to capture the attention of people scanning through publications. This is a function of design. You have to make the ad itself easy to scan using images, headlines, white space, appropriate typestyle and other design elements. However, the information in the ad must be of interest to those who will read it from top to bottom, keeping in mind (again!) your target market and the purpose of the ad.

Key # 8: Ask for action. Ask the reader to take action. You can do this subtly with a website address or toll-free number. Or you can motivate the reader to act using a variety of incentives.

Key #9: Suggest visuals. Every ad starts with a concept. The copy and visuals must work together to make the concept come alive. You don't have to be the Art Director to suggest visuals for the ad. Your headline might immediately suggest a visual. If it does not, share your vision with the Art Director or graphic designer. Also, suggest visuals to go with the ad—especially direct marketing brochures— such as charts, graphs or illustrations.

Chapter 10: The Poetry of Copywriting

Copywriting has become the poetry of our generation. On reflection, that is a sad thought. Allow me to rephrase it: Effective copywriting steals from poetry.

Take a moment and read this excerpt from the prose poem, *A Child's Christmas in Wales*, by Dylan Thomas. **Note**: the *italics* in the poem are mine.

> One *Christmas* was so much like another, in those years around the sea-town corner now and out of all sound except the distant speaking of the voices I sometimes hear a moment before sleep, that I can never remember whether it *snowed* for six days and six nights when I was *twelve* or whether it *snowed* for *twelve days* and *twelve nights* when I was six.
>
> All the *Christmases* roll down toward the two-tongued sea, like a *cold* and headlong moon *bundling* down the sky that was our street; and they stop at the *rim of the ice-edged fish-freezing waves* and I plunge my hands in the *snow* and bring out whatever I can find. In goes my hand into that *wool-white bell-tongued ball of holidays* resting at *the rim of the carol-singing sea* and out come Mrs. Prothero and the *firemen.*
>
> It was on the afternoon of the *Christmas Eve* and I was in Mrs. Prothero's garden, waiting for cats, with her son Jim. It was *snowing.* It was always *snowing* at *Christmas. December,* in my memory, is *white* as *Lapland,* though there were no *reindeers.* But there were cats. Patient, *cold* and callous, our *hands wrapped in socks,* we waited to *snowball* the cats. Sleek and long as jaguars and horrible-whiskered, spitting and snarling, they would slink and sidle over the *white* back-garden walls and the lynx-eyed hunters, Jim and I, *fur-capped* and moccasined trappers from Hudson Bay, off Mumbles Road, would hurl our deadly *snowballs* at the green of their eyes. The wise cats never appeared.
>
> We were so still, *Eskimo-footed arctic* marksmen in the *muffling* silence of the *eternal snows*—eternal, ever since Wednesday—that we never heard Mrs. Prothero's first cry from her *igloo* at the bottom of the

garden. Or, if we heard it at all, it was, to us, like the far-off challenge of our enemy and prey, the neighbour's *polar* cat. But soon the voice grew louder.

"*Fire!*" cried Mrs. Prothero and she beat the dinner-gong.

A poem tells its story through tightly woven images that relate to a central theme (concept or hook, if you will). All but two of the italicized words belong in the same thematic set that I'll label *winter* or *Christmas*. *Fire* and *fireman*, being hot, may be perceived as opposites. However, being opposites—like black is to white—they, too, relate. Think of *hot* as it relates to Christmas (which occurs in winter), and you might think of candles, Yule logs and lights. All thematically connected.

I do not mean to diminish poetry by comparing it to advertising. Nor am I attempting to elevate copywriting. As I have said, effective copywriting starts with a concept, a hook whose theme runs throughout the copy. Same with good poetry. This theme, this golden thread that runs from start to finish, is the poetry of copywriting.

In an ad, the images and words make this theme come alive for the reader. This is how you capture attention. By running the thematic thread from beginning to end—from headline, through subhead and body copy all the way to the slogan, the copywriter gently pulls the reader through the ad. This is how you maintain interest and influence attitude.

Of course, to be truly effective, all this happens while the ad relates to the reader's needs or desires (real, perceived, or created by the advertiser).

Clustering Revisited

Remember the clustering exercises you did? One of the objectives of clustering is to help you get down on paper all the words and phrases that you associate with the keyword, which we can now reveal as your concept. Clustering is meant to help you think without thinking, to help you create a thematic set of words that you can use in your copy.

Will you use all the words from your cluster? No. Will you add words that are not in your cluster? Most likely. Clustering gives you a starting point—a potentially poetic starting point at that. Any professional writer will tell you that they would rather start writing with something rather than nothing on the page.

At this point, feel free to revisit your VCVC ad. Did you develop a well-defined hook? Did your image, headline and body copy build on your theme or hook? Did all your copy speak to or relate to your target market's needs (or, in this instance, desire)? Or did you take it a step further—create a desire for the target market and associate VCVC with the fulfillment of that desire?

Feel free to go back and redo your VCVC ad once you complete this chapter. Even if you do not revise it, be sure to apply what you learn here when writing all future copy.

With all that in mind, review the copy from this Nissan Pathfinder ad:

Headline: If you want to rough it, turn off the air-conditioning

Body copy: Adventure has always been civilized in the 2002 Nissan Pathfinder. Available heated leather seats, automatic climate control, and a 6-disc CD Bosse audio system help keep that tradition alive. And as for power and capability, it comes with a 250-HP V6 engine and All-Mode 4WD, one of the most advanced 4WD systems in the world. It also won the J.D. Power and Associates Award for the "Best Midsize Sport Utility Vehicle in Initial Quality." So, next time you venture into savage terrain, bring some sophistication with you. For more information, visit a Nissan Dealership today or check out www.nissancanada.com.

Go through the copy and find or highlight the thematically linked words in the ad. Here's a hint: To establish the theme, start with the headline! Also, remember that opposites belong in the same thematic set.

What do you see when you look at the poetry of this ad? To whom is this ad speaking? What does the target market desire? What does the target market not want to give up? (See Chapter 27, Appendix III.)

Frankly, this ad rather reminds me of Monty Python's *The Vocational Guidance Counsellor Sketch* in which a chartered accountant goes to a vocational counsellor, seeking a career change. The counsellor tells him he is suited to be ... a chartered accountant.

Accountant: No! No! No! You don't understand. I've been a chartered accountant for the last twenty years. I want a new job. Something exciting that will let me live.

Counsellor: Well, do you have any idea of what you want to do?

Accountant: Yes, yes I have.

Counsellor: What?

Accountant: (boldly) Lion taming.

It turns out the accountant thinks that anteaters are lions, and when the counsellor describes a lion to the accountant, he quickly changes his mind and asks about a career in banking.

The point of the story? There is the person the target market aspires to be, and the person the target market is. It is your job to appeal to the former, without forgetting the latter. (In case you have not gone to Appendix III and are not quite getting it, look at the headline again. Do you see the opposites?) The extent to which you balance both is a conscious decision based on the target market, the product, and the purpose of the ad.

Look at beer commercials that play on the target market's desire for sex, sex, sex, and more sex. When your target market is male and 19 to 24, you can't go wrong focusing on sex—something the target market aspires to have. However, remembering that opposites are equal, some beer companies differentiate themselves by focusing on the opposite (as opposed to the opposite sex). Take the ads for Molson Export, commonly referred to as Molson X, that ran several years ago. They featured nerdy guys *who were having too much sex.* In the ad, they want to get away from their girlfriends so they could drink beer and bond. By using a 180-degree variation on the theme of desiring sex, Molson X differentiated its brand (brand differentiation is one way of establishing a USP) from many of the other mass-market beers out there.

Speaking of beer and brand differentiation, there are microbreweries that target an older and richer demographic. They focus on snob appeal (the desire to be perceived as above the fray) by advertising sophisticated taste, and the art and craft of brewing. Then there are the breweries that focus on price alone. They say they deliver quality—as good as all the other beers out there—for less. No sexual content is employed because market research indicated that there were enough beer drinkers who cared more about price than about drinking a brand associated with their fantasies. Based on that, a number of low-priced brands of beer have been successfully launched. Of course the major labels, with their market share eroding, are now fighting back based on price—trying to squash the USP of all these low-cost beers.

But with that, we are moving far away from the field of copywriting and into the fields of marketing and competition. The point is, the copywriter has to be armed with marketing information (remember the seven-stage marketing strategy?) if he or she is to develop effective ads.

Let us return to the Nissan ad copy for a moment. Notice how it takes for granted that the Nissan target market has a degree of knowledge about automobiles or SUVs. The copy uses *4WD* (instead of *four-wheel drive*) and *HP* (instead of *horsepower*). It quotes an authority, J.D. Power, without qualifying the authority (a global marketing information firm that conducts independent and unbiased surveys of customer satisfaction, product quality and buyer behaviour).

To qualify all of the above terms would be condescending and the target market for this vehicle would not find condescension at all flattering.

There are other ways the ad presumes the target market is automotive savvy. For instance, it describes *features*, not *assets* and *benefits*.

All-Mode 4WD is a feature. It is not an asset or benefit. It *has* these things, and if I knew more about cars, I could describe 4WD's qualities in depth. Let's assume though that 4WD provides you with the asset of better handling, especially on rough terrain. The implied benefit of "superior control, even over the worst terrain" really means "you won't crash or roll your expensive new SUV, so you'll look like a champ on or off the road." The target market knows this, therefore the copywriter doesn't have to spell it all out.

The *250-HP V6 engine* is also a feature, something tangible that the SUV possesses. Again, the assets and benefits are not spelled out. Same with *6-Disc CD Bosse Audio System*. The ad presumes that I know enough to know that Bosse is a solid name in audio and that a 6-Disc CD means I can play six CDs in order or put them on random play. How civilized!

If this were the first SUV on the market or the first vehicle to have a 6-Disc CD player, the advertiser would have to *educate* the consumer. Educating involves spelling out features, assets and benefits. However, once the target market has become familiar with the product category, the advertiser can get away with less.

Look at the following computer ad:

Vostro 3550

Outstanding Value

- 2nd generation Intel Core i7-2620M processor, 2.70 GHz with Turbo Boost 2.0 up to 3.40 GHz
- Genuine Windows 7 Professional, 64-bit, English
- Colour: Aberdeen Silver
- Productivity Software: Microsoft® Office Starter 2010
- Memory: 4GB DDR3 at 1333MHZ, 1 DIMM
- 500GB 7200RPM SATA Hard Drive
- Battery Options: 6-cell Lithium Ion Primary Battery
- LCD Display: 15.6 inch High Definition LED Display (1366 x 768) with anti-glare
- Camera and Digital Microphone: Integrated 2.0 MP FHD Webcam and Digital Array Mic with Dell Webcam Central
- Graphics Card: AMD Radeon HD 6630M (128-bit) 1GB Graphic

- Optical Drive: 8X DVD+/-RW with double-layer DVD+/-R write capability
- Wireless Card: Intel WiFi 1030 802.11 b/g/n/BT3.0 Combo

The only "copy" in this description is: *Outstanding Value*. The rest consists of features (also known as "specs")—tangible *stuff* about the computer. In the ad, there was a "save $100," and a system price as well.

This ad does not mean all consumers know the assets and benefits of each feature. It does not even mean that all consumers know what each feature is or does. It means that computers have become a commodity and that most advertisers sell based on features and price.

Consumers compare Vostro's features and prices to other systems sold at Best Buy, Future Shop, Radio Shack, Joe's Bargain Computer Depot, and yes, even at the Apple Store, and so on. If none of the information in the ad makes sense, they find friends or relatives who can help them make the right decision.

That kind of advertising leaves little room for creativity. However, there are times when computer advertisers get creative. This generally occurs when they are targeting a specific slice of the computer-buying public or they are trying to differentiate their company and/or products from the competition.

Look at the copy from a Dell computer ad that appeared in the *Toronto Star*: Prominently featured at the top of the ad, you see *a woman in a kitchen*. The woman is holding a Dell laptop. There is a caption identifying the woman as:

Trish Magwood, Owner, Dish Cooking Studio - Toronto, ON.
In business since 2000. 26 full- and part-time employees

Trish is an entrepreneur. A small businessperson. Notice that she is an "owner," not a CEO. She has recently started her business (the ad ran in 2004) but she already has 26 employees. Seems successful to me! And she uses Dell computers. She is a poster child representing the Dell's target market—entrepreneurs and small-business owners.

Target markets like to see themselves in advertising. Actually, not quite true. In most instances, people like to see those they aspire to be. For instance, a small-business owner aspires to be successful, so Dell shows a successful entrepreneur.

Now look at the slinky, airbrushed models in cosmetics ads. There are women who aspire to that look, achievable or not. (It must be achievable because the women in the ads have achieved it!)

Only recently are we starting to see real women in the Dove campaign for real beauty (www.campaignforrealbeauty.com). The jury is still out in terms of how effective the ads are, but the ads are generating a great deal of publicity and critical acclaim.

> **Publicity** - a public relations tool focused on generating media coverage for an organization and/or its products. Involves placing positive and newsworthy information about a business, its products, or its policies in the media. It can include the dissemination of promotional material to draw interest to ad campaigns.

Of course, one could write an entire book on how to generate publicity. Oh, wait, I did! (*How to Write Media Releases to Promote Your Business, Organization or Event*). But I digress. What I want to do is look at the copy in the Dell ad.

Headline:
"I always use fresh ingredients. So does Dell."

How does the headline relate to the image? What concept is at work here?

Now here is the body copy:

> Dish Cooking Studio Owner, Trish Magwood, knows that growing your business is a lot like preparing a fine meal: pay attention to detail, follow a proven recipe, and always use fresh ingredients. That's why this successful entrepreneur chooses Dell.

> "My PCs are an important ingredient to my business. I chose Dell because they offer the latest quality components and they rigorously test all of their systems. Plus, they don't build it until I buy it."

> The 4-year-old Toronto cooking school that has grown to include full-service catering and an upcoming television show, uses 8 Dell desktops to help manage a 6,000-customer database, online bookings and all administrative and financial applications.

> "I don't want outdated technology that's been sitting on a store shelf. My business cooks with quality ingredients. In my opinion, that's Dell."

Do you see how the ad copy supports the *concept*? Do you see how this concept is used to differentiate Dell from other computer manufacturers and speak to a specific slice of the computer-buying public at the same time? Of course, there are pictures of computers, computer system specs, prices, and information on how to order in the ad. The point here is that the ad tells a focused and compelling story that relates to a particular target market.

There might be some spill-over—consumers who do not run businesses would might still be impressed with this ad and might buy Dell. Nothing wrong with that, if it occurs. However, the ad itself is focused on small businesses and entrepreneurs. Not the consumer. Not large enterprises. But small businesses. And it delivers enough information so that the target market can make a purchase decision.

Now let's return to the Pathfinder copy for a moment. You can look at the copy and ask: But does it sell Pathfinders? Good question. After reading the ad, would you run out and buy a Pathfinder? If you were not in the market for a new vehicle, or if you were in the market for a gas-efficient vehicle, you would probably not even read the ad. No problem because you are not the target market. However, let us say for a moment that you are looking for a new vehicle and that you are particularly interested in an SUV. Does this ad sell you? If so, how? If not, why not?

In short, what is the purpose of this particular ad? Is the purpose of this ad to generate immediate sales? If you wanted your target market to buy now, what would you do differently? Or is the purpose meant to create brand awareness, to get the target market thinking about Nissan so that when the target market is ready to buy, he or she at least visits a Nissan dealership?

All points to ponder as we move forward.

Chapter 11: Advertising's Environment

While poor advertising is often blamed for a company's failure, and effective advertising is sometimes credited with a company's success, advertising actually serves a limited role, one that is integrated within the *business environment*.

We looked briefly at the business environment when we were discussing the marketing plan. The business environment is the external environment — economic, social/cultural, technological, political and legal—in which the business operates.

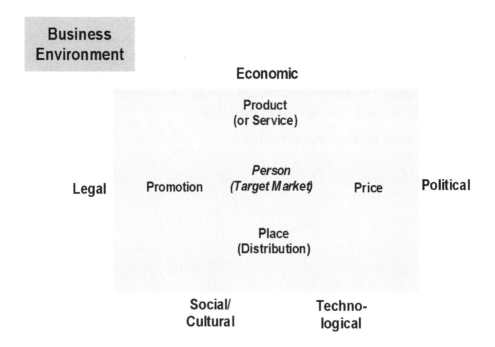

The anti-tobacco lobby (social/cultural) put pressure on the political system. Subsequently, laws were passed to ban tobacco advertising, as well as to restrict where people can smoke. It is not illegal to operate a tobacco manufacturing company or to sell cigarettes (as long as they are sold to people over the age of 19, at least in Ontario, where I live).

However, the business environment is making it difficult for companies to be in the cigarette industry. Thank heavens cigarettes are addictive, or the big tobacco companies would all be out of business! Into that environment steps the copywriter. Actually, because it is illegal to advertise cigarettes, at least in some countries, the copywriter might not step into *that* environment. Instead, let us take a look at the news about *trans fats*.

There are countless articles about trans fats in newspapers and magazines. Evidently, they are not good for you. Not as bad as cigarettes, maybe, because they have not been restricted. There are calls to ban them, but until that happens you can still eat a cookie containing trans fats in public. However, consumers are getting the message: *trans fats = poor health*.

If your client makes cookies or food products that contain trans fats, there is not much that you, as the copywriter, can do. Obviously, you don't play up the fact that the food product contains trans fats. In fact, you don't mention it. But the information belongs on the packaging (a political decision, in response to social pressures, with legal implications). No matter what you write, you cannot arrest declining sales if consumers are resistant to trans fats.

Look at the business environment illustration again. The copywriter has no control over the external environment in which the company and its products exist. The copywriter does not control the features of the product. He or she does not control the price of the product nor the place where the product is sold.

The copywriter does not control which elements of the promotion or marketing mix will be used. *The copywriter writes the copy.*

Now, given an environment in which trans fats are considered bad for you, and given a product that has eliminated trans fats, the copywriter would be a fool if he or she did not take advantage of the situation and write a headline like:

> Because no kid ever said,
> *"Hey Mom, can I have some more trans fat?"*

The ad, for Spudz Stix, uses a friendly typeface in the headline—it almost looks like a child has scribbled, neatly, mind you, the headline on the ad. We can also admire the use of two colours—one for the *because* line (red) and one for the *quote* (blue). But that would be admiring the designer's work. Let's, instead, admire the copywriter's work.

- What has the copywriter done here? Why?
- Whom is the copywriter talking to? Why?
- Why does the headline start with "Because"?

Go back to the seven-stage marketing plan and see if you can recreate elements of the plan the copywriter was working from. In other words, try to reverse engineer the ad to see if you can find the foundation upon which the concept is built. But before you do that, look at the body copy and slogan....

Body Copy:
New Spudz Stix are air-popped, not fried, and contain zero trans fats. Of course the only thing kids care about is that they're delicious. They come in great flavours like Ketchup, Cheesy Nacho, and Ranch – and they're from Quaker, so Mom's going to love them too.

Slogan:
The only thing kids know is that they're delicious

Of course, there was a big picture of the Spudz Stix package in the ad too.

After you review the marketing plan, look at the copy in relation to the twenty tips and the nine keys presented earlier in the book. Try to determine which tips and keys it follows and which ones it doesn't—and why it does or doesn't follow the various tips and keys.

To help you assess the ad, ask if the copy:

- Knows the audience
- Uses language the target market understands
- Uses a great headline
- Makes an impact and strikes a nerve
- Magnetizes or draws customers to the product
- Demonstrates product knowledge
- Uses short sentences and runs from pompous words
- Educates, not sells
- Focuses on benefits
- Focuses on the client
- Conveys a particular image
- Brings out personality
- Flows logically (is organized)
- Demonstrates consistency

Also, does the copy:

- Start with the prospect (target market) in mind?
- Gain attention?

- Make the ad FABulous—Features, Assets, Benefits?
- Differentiate the product from the competition?
- Be the 3 C's: Clear, Compelling, Conversational?
- Overcome objections, suspicion, and doubt?
- Involve writing for readers, but format or design for scanners?
- Ask for action?
- Suggest (include) visuals?

And to all that, might I add: Is the copy poetic? Can you find a theme woven throughout the copy?

Countless other ads are in tune with some or all aspects of the business environment. Look for and analyze ads that are in tune with aspects of the business environment. This kind of analysis will help you understand that the job of the copywriter is to do more than string pithy words and statements together. The job of the copywriter is to understand the business environment and the marketing strategy, and then to develop a concept that makes sense within that environment and strategy. Then string pithy words and statements together, using what we've called *poetry*, in a way that captures attention of the right person for the right reason, holds interest, influences attitude, and causes the reader to act— even though that action might not be to buy. It could be as simple as to feel good about a product or to remember the next time the reader needs it.

It is not the copywriter's job to determine what the business environment or marketing strategy for the product is. Those are strategic marketing decisions— often made based on research and the analysis of sales and various business trends. But once the decision is made to incorporate (or not incorporate) business environment factors into an ad or ad campaign, the copywriter needs to know what the decision is, which of the business environment factors are in play, why the decision was made, and how the product or service relates to these factors. And, of course, the writer must understand the marketing strategy that marketing has determined will best help the company promote or sell the product, raise brand awareness, or cause the consumer to associate the product with a particular idea, image or feeling.

Without that marketing input from the client (or employer, if the writer is working for an in-house agency or advertising department), the copywriter is attempting to shoot fish in the ocean. He or she might get lucky, but will more likely completely miss the mark.

Chapter 12: From Branding to Hard Sell

Advertising agencies make big bucks working on branding campaigns. The value of a brand is often overblown, but there is no denying that many consumers are attracted by the familiar. If a brand becomes familiar enough, consumers will gravitate to it. Even iconoclasts like the familiar. Look at how Naomi Klein's book, *No Logo,* has become a brand for those opposing globalization. You might say that *the familiar* of the iconoclast is different than *the familiar* of those who cherish traditional beliefs, institutions and brands. But it is still familiar.

For instance, in the mid-1980s, iconoclasts started to drink Black Label, a beer that had done little more than gather dust on beer store shelves for a decade or more. They began to drink it because they wore black and the label on Black Label is black, and because nobody else—save for a few old-timers in Legion Halls—was drinking it.

Then the marketers discovered this new trend and informed the creative directors and copywriters. The creative director created dark Black Label ads and the copywriters wrote counterculture copy. The beer underwent a renaissance—because, at heart, we all want to be iconoclasts. The true iconoclasts, disgusted that the rest of us were jumping on their bandwagon, soon stopped drinking Black Label. The brand lost its cachet, again, and soon nobody was drinking it—other than loyal Legion members. At least in Canada.

However, in the United Kingdom, Black Label is best known for a series of ads showing people doing cool, clever or difficult things. A bystander says, "I bet he drinks Carling Black Label."

Largely because of this ad campaign, Black Label has been the best-selling brand of beer in Britain since 1971, *although it is not particularly well regarded by beer aficionados.* But then, what does taste have to do with drinking beer? Everything if you are a beer aficionado; nothing if you want to be perceived of as cool by bystanders.

Where does that leave the copywriter? If you, as copywriter, do not know how the advertiser wants its target market to perceive the brand (think and feel about the brand), how can you write the words required to create that brand impression?

But all that leads to the question: What is a brand?

> **Branding** can be described as the process by which a brand identity is developed. The **brand** is the unique *awareness* and *memory* a potential customer has of the products or services offered.

A brand is intangible, but—like memory—it feels real—as real as the words, graphics, or symbols that are associated with the products or services offered by a business.

Look at symbols and logos that represent well-known brands. Think of the Nike swoosh, McDonald's golden arches, iconic Coca Cola or IBM logos. Jot down what you think or feel (your brand impression) as you look at or think about them. I'm not saying that your thoughts will be positive; I am saying you will have thoughts.

Some logos are so powerful and synonymous with their brands—like McDonald's golden arches or the Nike swoosh—that they require no words to make the reader think of the brand when they see the logo.

However, it takes millions and millions and millions of marketing dollars (and many words and images) to burn a particular association between a logo and the product or company into the consumer's mind.

While advertisers try to create brand associations and brand awareness, they cannot control your thoughts. Or can they?

Until she turned 12, my daughter loved to eat at McDonald's. Something funny happened when she was in grade seven (the year she turned 12). She was hanging out with a group of friends and one said that she had heard that there were not enough cows in the world to make all the burgers McDonald's served. The company, she said, had to use filler. And the filler they used? *Worms*!

That story is, of course, an urban myth. However, by telling the story to her peers, an iconoclast had turned a group of once-loyal customers against the product. The brand image was shattered. My daughter has not eaten at McDonald's since. But how can a copywriter, or an entire marketing department, combat and overcome such negative word of mouth? They cannot.

My daughter no longer believes that McDonald's uses worms in their burgers. However, something happened that day. She became a more discriminating consumer. With the brand's lustre tarnished, she moved out of the McDonald's target market range, as did many of her friends. My relief was palpable when my daughter said she no longer wanted to eat at McDonald's. I know many other parents who were also quite relieved.

How did McDonald's react to the fact that many of its customers were growing up and abandoning the brand (not because of the worm story, but because they were becoming older, wiser and more discriminating consumers)? How did McDonald's react to the fact that many parents were particularly happy (given the social/cultural changes in eating habits) to give up Big Macs?

McDonald's did several things. It changed its menu, adding lighter fare, including salads. It changed its slogan to *I'm lovin' it*. And it changed the music associated with the brand to an edgier hip-hop beat, without going so edgy as to offend those customers who remained loyal. Even its commercials changed: out with the Happy Meals, in with older folks (not *old* folks, but folks *older* than its previous demographic)—all lovin' the new menu at McDonald's. None of that means McDonald's is out of the woods, but the company's fortunes have improved. Fact is, due to an ever-changing business environment, no company is ever out of the woods.

So, to reiterate, there is a great deal copywriters do not control. However, there is much copywriters must know (even about those things that they do not control) before they can produce the kind of copy that projects the brand or image a company wants to project. And there is even more the copywriter must know if he or she is going to use copy to sell something—to actually get the target audience to take action.

Look at the ad below, and then we will look at branding versus hard sell from a copy perspective.

Born and raised in Funkytown.

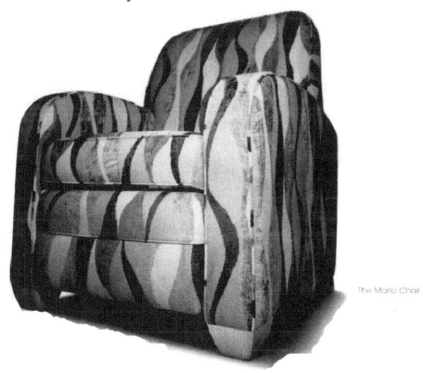

The Marlo Chair

The new look of comfort'

Headline: *Born and raised in Funkytown.*
Slogan (below the logo): *The new look of comfort.*

La-Z-boy was founded in 1927. I remember my father reclining in his La-Z-Boy rocker. I turned 50 years old in 2004, and I'm writing this in 2005. Why is that important? There is a saying in advertising: You cannot sell consumers their parents' products. But you can sell them their grandparents' products. And that is exactly what La-Z-Boy is doing here. Okay, *sell* is too strong a word. The company is *repositioning* its brand for a new generation of consumers by giving it a new, funky look.

I am not that generation. My children are.

The song, Funkytown, was released in 1979. It hit the charts in 1980. While some Baby Boomers (people like me) may have discoed to it, the song belonged to a different generation. That generation was old enough to invest in decent furniture (instead of shopping at Goodwill) in 2003, when this La-Z-Boy ad was produced. The ad might cause a few folks to run out and purchase La-Z-Boy chairs. More than likely, it caused those who danced to Funkytown in 1980 to start humming. And if an ad can get you humming (or laughing or crying or swearing), it has engaged you or captured your attention. That is about all most ads—especially positioning or branding ads—can hope to do.

So how do you sell someone something?

Branding Versus Hard Sell

One of the many things copywriters need to know is the purpose or objective of the ad. For instance, is the purpose to position a brand or create brand awareness? Or is the purpose of the ad to sell?

How many La-Z-Boy chairs moved off the shelf the day the above ad ran? Very few, I'd guess.

So how do you sell a product like La-Z-Boy? That you leave up to the retailer. In other words, the above ad is meant to position the product as funky to a new generation, and create awareness within a defined segment of the furniture-buying market. It is not meant to motivate people to buy. There is no call to action and no incentive to shop now.

However, when La-Z-Boy Furniture Galleries runs its Great Rebate Event ad in the *Toronto Star*, it is expected that La-Z-Boy chairs and other furniture will move by the truckload!

Here is some of the copy from the La-Z-Boy Furniture Galleries Great Rebate Event ad:

La-Z-Boy Furniture Galleries

Great Rebate Event

HURRY!

SALE ENDS TOMORROW!

Up to $150 in savings

NO PAYMENTS, NO INTEREST FOR UP TO 1 YEAR!

La-Z-Time Full Reclining Chaise Sofa

Reg. $1349

- $37 La-Z-Boy Instant Rebate

- $37 In-Store Rebate

$1274 AFTER REBATES

100s of Models in Stock for Immediate Delivery!

There are four other products featured at sale or rebate prices. Of course, the ad included the address of La-Z-Boy Furniture Gallery outlets, store hours, phone numbers, maps to stores and a website address. Oh, in case you don't have enough cash in your pocket, there are images of the Visa, MasterCard and Interac logos.

Now do you feel motivated to buy something? If you feel good about the La-Z-Boy brand and are in the market for a new chair, you just might be motivated to buy. After all, you only have one day left to save, save, save!

Do you see the difference between brand positioning and hard sell? Do you see why it is important to know the purpose of the ad, among the other things we've discussed, before writing copy? Do you see why branding copy is so much more fun, from a creative perspective, to write? But why hard-sell copy moves product?

To move products such as La-Z-Boy chairs, however, the company first had to build brand awareness and position the product. Then it could essentially sit back and leave the rest of the selling to its retailers.

So does copy have to be retail hard-sell to motivate people to buy? No, not always. When we look at Direct Response Marketing (Chapters 15 to 19), we'll see that we do not have to use retail hard-sell to motivate people to take action. But to be effective, we still have to motivate people to take action.

Chapter 13: Writing Copy

Is there always time, or need, to review the marketing plan and to discuss in detail the target market and purpose? Need, yes. Time, no. But do try to find or make time to gather as much information as possible. If you are writing catalogue copy, however, about the only thing you need to know (beyond the product features) is whether the product is on sale.

Most catalogue copy consists of short descriptions of numerous products sold through retail chains such as Best Buy, Future Shop, Canadian Tire, Sears, The Bay, J.C. Penny, and so on. The headline is often nothing more than the product name. The copy consists of a few features and the price. If the product is on sale, the word *Save!* (or some variation on it, such as *Half-Price* or *Why Wait?*) might be part of the headline or the first words used in the copy block.

As dull as I am trying to make catalogue copywriting sound, there is room—sometimes—for a little creative flair.

Look at these two blocks of copy. Which do you think piques the interest of the reader more? Why?

> **Fruit and Vegetable Cushion**. Place this unique cushion in your fridge box and the porous construction of the mat will allow air to circulate all round—preventing mould—while cushioning your vegetables against bruising. Why not try it in your fruit basket? What a difference it will make. Can be cut to size. 11-1/4" x 18-1/2". $9.95

Are you inspired? Do you want one? Are you at all interested? Might you try it in your fruit basket? Or are you totally put off fruits and veggies, thinking about all that mould? Now read the copy as written a year later:

> **Fruit and Vegetable Cushion**. Are you able to buy fresh fruit and vegetables every day? If not, any help you can get to improve storage is welcome. The cushioning effect and porous construction of this special matting allows air to circulate, preventing mould and bruising. Place it in the base of your fridge box or fruit bowl to keep your fruits and vegetables fresh. Can be cut to size. 11-1/4" x 18-1/2". $9.95

Are you any more, or less, interested? Why? Which copywriter tried to imagine and connect with a target market? How? Which one makes the reader feel that they may have discovered a solution to a problem they did not even know they had? Which one speaks to the reader directly? How?

Read both blocks again. This time when you read, differentiate between the features, the tangible aspects of the products, and any listed assets and benefits.

Write Copy for....

To help you write several copy blocks, look at the products and services below. They include exaggerated features to help you have fun with spelling out the benefits. The features may seem a tad silly, but this is an exercise in expressing yourself creatively using ad copy.

To start, pick at least one product (but feel free to pick several) and define your target market for that product.

Once that is done, define your purpose for the ad you are going to write.

To loosen up your creativity and to help you find the hook on which you can hang your copy, try some of the creative writing exercises used earlier in this book, and that were used when writing the VCVC ad. Do some clustering and try a few freefalls. Look at the product from the perspective of the target market and from the perspective of those who would have no interest in the product.

Once you go through some of the creative exercises and find your hook, produce an idea for an image and write a headline that connects with your image. In short, make your concept real.

Then review the copywriting tips and keys in Chapter 9, list the copy points you feel you should address in your copy, to meet your purpose, and write a copy block.

To review, for each product or service you choose, do the following:
- Determine your target market
- Determine your purpose
- Come up with a concept
- Select an image and write a headline (and/or subhead) to make your concept real
- List your copy points you should cover
- Write a short copy block (25-to-100 words).

Again, feel free to try this for some of, or all of, the products below. The most important thing you can do is apply the process—from creative brainstorming to mining for concepts, to linear outlining, to writing with poetry in mind.

Product List

1. **WriteOn!** A sleek, stylish, personally monogrammed, 14-karat gold, platinum-tipped executive fountain pen that never runs out of ink. Retail price: $995.

2. **CrashFree PC.** A family-friendly computer that never crashes (continues to work even if Junior spills pop on the keyboard!). It can be left on all the time. Powers down into ultra-energy-saver mode when not used for 10 minutes. You'll never have to boot up again.

3. **Taxing Incentives.** A new consumer and small-business tax preparation company that guarantees the accuracy of your return. If they make an error, they pay 100% of the difference on your behalf; competitive rates with H&R Block.

4. **Full in Five.** An organization that aims to convince first-world governments to end world hunger in five years needs to raise funds.

5. **Ch0c0late.** A decadently delicious, fat-free, sugar-free, calorie-free, premium chunky chocolate ice cream that costs no more than Häagen-Dazs.

6. **Magnetique.** A French designer perfume so in tune with your innermost desires that the fragrance attracts only those you are interested in and repels the creeps.

7. **You.** Create an ad that lands you the job of your dreams.

You may have questions about the products, the kind of questions that are answered in a marketing plan. Feel free to answer them and to create your own features, assets and benefits. In short, have fun and write some stellar, creative ad copy.

Same Product—Different Target Market

Can you sell the same product to different target markets? Absolutely. There will often be spill-over from one ad to different target markets (as we saw with the Dell computer ad), but if you want to target two distinct markets, you need to produce two distinct ads. In other words, do you simply want to mop up some spill-over, or do you want to spend additional marketing dollars to reach both target markets?

For instance, what if your market research indicates that the occasional health-food fanatic breaks down and sneaks into McDonald's for a Big Mac? Do you start running McDonald's ads in *Vitality*, a lifestyle magazine for people into health foods, yoga, and new-age philosophy? Probably not. You could spend a lot of money, and not sell many more burgers. But what if you find a significant number of seniors on fixed incomes dine at fast-food restaurants at least once a week. You might want to run targeted ads in publications that reach seniors.

Why targeted ads? I don't think Happy Meal ads would cut it in a publication like *Today's Senior*—unless you worked in a special discount for grandparents who brought their grandchildren to McDonald's.

Some companies must sell the same product to different target markets. Take the manufacturers of our fictitious pop, VCVC, for instance. While it makes sense for the company to target the demographic spelled out in the marketing strategy (in Chapter 8), the company also has to get the product into convenience stores.

All the advertising in the world will not sell VCVC if the product is not placed (distributed) where the target market can easily reach it. Therefore, the company has to sell it to convenience store chains and owners of mom & pop operations. This is a far different target market than those who will actually drink VCVC.

While VCVC Co. might use direct sales—sending salespeople to speak to convenience store chain product managers and owners of mom & pop operations—the company would probably soften them up (make them *aware* of the product) by placing ads in trade magazines read by convenience store executives, managers, and mom & pop store owners.

> **Trade magazine**: A publication dedicated to the interests of a specific trade or industry, often providing such information as news of the field, descriptions of products and services, lists of new publications, legislative activities and so on.

Their ads might run in convenience store industry trade magazines. Alternatively, VCVC might send a direct mail (direct response marketing or DRM) sales letter or brochure to their convenience store target market.

Will a business-to-business ad meant to convince convenience stores to carry VCVC (to create space on shelves and in fridges already crowded with a variety of brands of soda pop) differ from one aimed at the consumer? Absolutely. Different target market; different purpose; different message.

It takes a right-brain, or creative, ad to position the VCVC brand in the mind of consumers—to associate the product with a desire or some kind of memorable concept. However, it will take a left-brain, or linear, sales approach to reach the convenience store owners and managers. Think about what such an ad must do. It must appeal to the desire to boost profits, overcome objections, and most likely offer incentives to sell the product to convenience stores.

That does not mean that the copywriter should abandon creative exercises or ingenuity. You still need a hook and landmark words that capture the attention of the target market. But to hold the reader's interest, you have to write in a more linear, or business-like, manner. In other words, the tone of the ad will change.

> **Tone**: The writer's attitude toward his readers and his subject. A writer can be formal, informal, playful, ironic, optimistic or pessimistic. A formal tone may be business-like, while an informal tone may encourage a friendly, intimate feeling.

Some ads try to appeal to both the left and right side of a reader's brain, although they generally do it in a manner that pokes a little fun at the advertising industry. For instance, there was a two-page ad for Saab that played on this. Each page looked like a complete ad.

On the left page, the headline read as followed:

A CAR FOR THE LEFT SIDE
OF YOUR BRAIN

On the right page, the headline read as followed.

A CAR FOR THE RIGHT SIDE
OF YOUR BRAIN

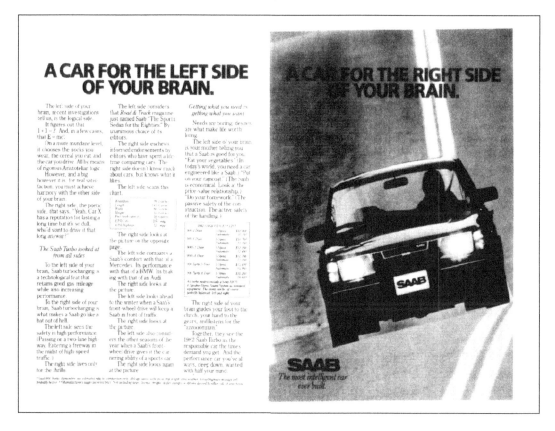

I know you can't read the copy in the above ad, but that is not important. Notice, instead, how the ad on the left side is copy heavy and even includes a couple of tables. The copy is meant to appeal to the logical, linear, or left-brain, reader. On the right side? Nothing but the headline, logo and slogan—"The most intelligent car ever built." And, of course, a large picture of a Saab. All meant to appeal to the creative, or right, side of the brain.

The emotional buyers, the ones who value style over substance, are reassured that they are getting style. But the substance doesn't hurt. The logical buyers, the ones who value substance over style, are reassured that they are getting substance. But the style doesn't hurt, either.

Don't feel you have to appeal to both sides of the brain when you write ads. You do, however, need to know what your reader needs to know, and then write your copy with that in mind.

Meanwhile, Back at VCVC....

Here you are, a brand-new soda pop producer. You are planning this lavish brand-awareness campaign, when suddenly it hits you—you have to get your pop into stores, or consumers who want to buy VCVC will not be able to do so. But, before you send your sales staff out knocking on doors, you want to create some awareness about your product.

Make a list of copy points that you would include in a VCVC ad intended to introduce convenience store owners to the pop. Think about running a one-page ad in a trade magazine meant to build brand awareness. The ad would contain all the elements in the Lion ad on page 40, so room for copy is limited.

Check your copy point list twice. Then try to think more creatively—come up with your concept, image and headline. What you would do to capture the attention of your target market? Feel free to do some brainstorming here.

Are we putting the cart before the horse—copy points before the creative? Yes and no. There is nothing wrong with having a list of the copy points you have to hit, before you develop your concept. In fact, many writers prefer to have their body copy roughed out before they develop the concept. Then, once they have the concept, headline and image in place, they revise the body copy—weaving in the poetic theme. You will find the way that works best for you.

In fact, one day one way might work for you; another day the other way might work better. It could depend on your mood, the product, the target market, or the purpose of the ad. Don't question it. Just harness either process as best you can.

Now let's expand our job. What if, instead of sending out a large sales force, you could motivate convenience store owners to call you and order VCVC? That would be cool, no? With that in mind, think about writing a DRM (direct response marketing) brochure (also known as a direct mail brochure—a brochure that you would mail directly to your target market).

Before you outline your copy points, think about your purpose. *You are trying to motivate action.* But this is not the "half-price, buy now" retail approach to motivating action. So what do you have to say to get your target market to act?

Think about some of the problems or objections your audience may have. How can you overcome them?

Before you answer that, you might be asking why you have to overcome them. Allow me to answer:

If you cannot overcome objections (influence the attitude of the reader), your audience will not act. It is that simple. I am a small "l" liberal, but if the Liberal Party of Canada wants my vote, it has to influence my attitude—in this case reinforce an attitude that is supportive—even though I am predisposed to vote Liberal. Why do you think voters who support particular parties often stay home on election day? The party has done little or nothing to influence voter attitude. How much harder do you think you have to work to convince someone who is predisposed to vote against you to vote for you? How hard do you think you have to work to sell something to somebody who has objections?

However, if you cannot capture attention and hold interest to begin with, your audience will not be there to have their attitude influenced by you. So let me repeat the question:

> Think about some of the objections your target market might have.
> What can you say to overcome them?

Now let me rephrase it slightly:

> Think about some of the problems your target market might have.
> What solutions do you have to offer?

Once you have the answers to those questions, you are well on your way to writing the body of your direct response brochure—a brochure meant to motivate your audience to act.

We will explore DRM in greater detail in Chapters 15 to 19. Right now, spend a bit of time thinking about how DRM differs from ads that are meant to do little more than build brand awareness. And think about the implications for the copy, and for the copywriter.

Chapter 14: The Communications Process

Before we look at direct response marketing, let's take a moment to review the Communications Process. Just as writing is a process, so is communications. Communications requires a *sender* who sends a *message* through a *channel* to a *receiver*. It seems a simple enough process:

1. I have information.
2. I put it in an email.
3. I send it to you.
4. You receive it.

How does that apply to advertising?

1. I have information about a product.
2. I create an ad and publish it.
3. You buy the publication.
4. You read it.

And that is how we communicate. Communication is a process. If you want to communicate effectively—in writing or when speaking—you should understand the process.

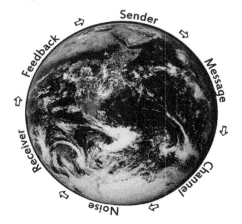

Communication requires a *sender* who sends a *message* through a *channel* to a *receiver*. The process is not complete, however, without *feedback*. Feedback closes the communication loop. Sometimes, *noise* (competing messages, distractions, misunderstandings) interferes with your message; feedback lets you know if the receiver received and understood your message.

When you communicate in person, you can ask for feedback: ask people if they understood or have any questions. However, when you communicate in writing or other one-way media (such as broadcast), it is more difficult to ask for feedback. Advertisers have learned how to use direct response marketing techniques such as discount coupons, time-limited offers and so on to motivate and measure feedback

Why Feedback?

Why would any sender, such as an advertiser, want feedback? And what constitutes feedback?

Advertisers want feedback when they communicate so they can measure the effectiveness of promotions. If they don't know how effective promotional campaigns are, how will they know whether they should run the same ads again, modify them, or scrap them and come up with something new? In short, advertisers use feedback to close the communications loop and complete the communications process. The nature of the feedback desired depends on the purpose of the ad.

It may seem obvious, but allow me to state it anyway: If you don't know how effective your ad campaign was, how will you know whether you should run it again (in other words, spend more money on it)? How will you know if you should make adjustments to your ad?

Why can't the sender simply presume that the receiver has received the message? As mentioned, sometimes noise thwarts the communications process.

Where might noise thwart the receipt of the message if the receiver is:
- Watching TV?
- Listening to the radio?
- Reading a print publication?
- On the web?
- Receiving email?

I'm sure you've come up with a number of noise factors, such as:
- Using the remote to change channels when commercials come on
- Talking to someone while the radio is playing and not hearing the commercial
- Closing a pop-up ad before reading it or clicking on a free search-engine listing rather than a paid ad
- Having a spam filter delete legitimate electronic newsletters or direct e-mail that the receiver has requested

The fact is, sometimes—often—your advertising message does not get through. It is the advertiser's job to solicit feedback so he or she can determine if the ad was effective. Often, the task of creating the copy that solicits feedback lands in the lap of the copywriter. You cannot eliminate all the noise that might interfere with the communications process; however, there are things you can do to solicit feedback and measure the effectiveness of an ad. But first you must know the purpose of the ad and the medium that the ad will appear in. Then you devise ways of soliciting feedback.

The means used to solicit feedback often change based on the medium and the message—at least the purpose of the message.

For instance, how might the means of soliciting feedback change if an advertiser sent an electronic newsletter to an email list rather than a direct mail flyer to a mailing list? How might the means used to solicit feedback change based on purpose—for instance, brand awareness versus sales?

If an advertiser sent an electronic newsletter to an email list, the advertising might request that readers click on a link to a website. Count the clicks, and you have feedback on your request. An advertiser who sends a direct mail flyer to a mailing list might ask recipients instead to call a toll-free number.

An advertiser who wants to solicit feedback based on an ad meant to raise brand awareness might survey a segment of the target market before and after the ad runs to determine if the ad has raised awareness. An advertiser interested in sales may look at sales and even store traffic on the day the ad runs, and for a few days afterwards.

Gauging Versus Motivating

It all seems pretty obvious. If the purpose of the ad is to motivate an action like visiting a website, then hits on the website constitute feedback. If the purpose is to get the audience to call for more information, then calls for more information constitute feedback. Likewise, if the purpose of an ad is to sell a product, then sales constitute your feedback. Run the ad and watch your sales. If they go up while the ad is running, deem it a successful ad. If they remain the same or go down, deem it a flop.

But how do you know if your sales increase is tied to the ad? What if you sell umbrellas and it rains the day your ad appears? If sales go up, do you attribute the sales increase to a stellar ad or to poor weather? How can you be sure? How can you accurately gauge feedback?

Allow me to now rephrase the question, because gauging feedback is not as important as motivating it. Oh, gauging is important. But if you do not motivate it, you will have little feedback to gauge. So, instead of asking how you can gauge feedback, answer me this: *How do you motivate feedback, such as sales*?

Motivating sales is different than gauging sales. Gauging sales is passive. Motivating sales is active. When you gauge sales, you find ways of relating sales to the ad. When you motivate sales, you use incentives to persuade people to give you feedback (take a defined action such as *buy something*).

Before you can motivate action, you have to capture attention, maintain interest and influence attitude, as we have said. But if you want action, it is your job to motivate it—to give your target market an *incentive* to act.

Incentives will be discussed in detail in the direct response marketing chapters, but start thinking about them now. How can you motivate people to buy (or to take some other defined action)? And how can you gauge feedback to see if your motivation worked?

The two—incentives that motivate and gauging feedback—are, as you will soon see, interconnected.

Sell Something

Return to the copy you wrote for WriteOn!, CrashFree PC, Taxing Incentives Inc., Full in Five, Ch0c0late, Magnetique, and You (in Chapter 13). Does your copy allow you to gauge feedback? Does your copy motivate the reader to any action? Are there any incentives in your copy that motivates readers to take any action?

Before you read on, determine how you will gauge feedback and motivate action, and then revise the copy for each of the above products. Provide a reason or incentive for the reader to act sooner rather than later. Do this without reading any further. See what you can do based on your gut instinct.

Motivating Sales

There are a number of ways you can motivate sales, and we will look at them in action in the next chapter. However, allow me to outline a few techniques that you can use. See if you can apply them, or one that feels most appropriate, to the "sell something" work you did, above. The technique you choose depends on your target audience, your purpose and your medium.

Tools for motivating the completion of the feedback loop in the communications process include:

- **Discount Coupons**. Consumers like to do things, like clipping coupons. So ads often include coupons that offer a certain dollar amount or percentage off, or two for the price of one. The coupons must be redeemed by a set time—that is the *incentive* to act now.

- **Free Sample.** This might be used in conjunction with a coupon, a toll-free number or a website. You give away a bag of chips in the hope that the consumer will, over time, buy dozens or hundreds. Bring in the coupon, call the toll-free number, or visit the website and fill out the form, and get a free sample. Of course, these are time-limited offers.

- **Free Product.** Give away a cell phone or home alarm system to motivate the consumer to sign up for a three-year plan. There might not be a coupon, but the offer will expire by a certain time—all to motivate the consumer to act within a specified period of time.

- **Free Quote or Estimate**. The free quote or estimate is usually a no-obligation offer. Depending on the product, it may be limited by time, but often is not.

- **Free Delivery**. Online shopping is increasing daily. Often, one of the main objections to shopping online is the delivery fee. So offer free delivery. You might offer it for a short period of time to entice people to try your product, or you might offer it on sales over a certain dollar value.

- **Free Trial**. Often used when selling software online. The trial software might not include all the features of the commercial package, or it might operate for 30 days. Give away the first four months of a magazine subscription to motivate the consumer to sign up for a year—all the consumer has to do is mail in the subscription form or subscribe online.

- **Contests**. You can call a toll-free number, visit a website or send in an email to enter the contest. Or you can visit the store and fill out a ballot. The contest should appeal to the target market and relate to the product or services (or season in which the ad appears). Again, don't forget the time-limited offer.

- **Money Back Guarantee**. Life is risky. We eliminate the risk with a 100% money-back guarantee. This is not so much an incentive to act now as it is a way to build trust. All the incentives in the world will not work, unless the consumer trusts the advertiser.

Keep your eyes on the lookout for other interesting offers meant to motive action. If you see something that works for your product or service, modify it and use it.

Chapter 15: Direct Response Marketing

As we have seen, the purpose of advertising is not necessarily to sell a product or service. However, there are times when generating the sale (or a lead for high-end, complex products) is paramount. When the purpose of the ad is to close the sale or generate a specific response, advertisers frequently turn to direct response marketing (DRM).

DRM, also known as direct response advertising or direct marketing, is a direct communication to a customer or business. Using mail, email, phone, fax or other media—including newspapers, trade magazines and information commercials (often seen on late-night TV), DRM is designed to generate a response in the form of an order, a request for further information, or a visit to a store or other place of business, such as a website. That response (or feedback) closes the communications loop and lets the advertiser know how effective (or ineffective) the DRM advertisement was.

To be effective, DRM must include all the information necessary to lead the prospect directly to an action, including the *call to action*. As we shall see, the DRM call to action frequently includes incentives to motivate the target market to *act now*!

Call to Action: A marketing and sales device that tells the customer how to take the next step towards a purchase or execute an activity. Often accompanied by a time-limited incentive to act.

Hook, Line and Sinker

The direct marketing brochure is generally printed in full colour on glossy stock. Often it runs several pages long and may include special die-cuts or folds. It is frequently mailed to the target market (often accompanied by a sales letter). It also, however, can be inserted in a magazine destined to reach the desired target market.

These days, many advertisers are cutting the costs of DRM by using email. Email used for marketing purposes is not spam—*as long as the recipient has given the mailer permission to send such email*. Permission-based email eliminates the cost of printing brochures and dramatically cuts the cost of mailing. (We will look at permission-based DRM email later in this chapter.)

The DRM sales letter, brochure or email lands right in the hands (or in-box) of the target market. But that does not mean the target market will read it. DRM pieces still have to capture the attention and hold the interest of the target market. To do so, DRM uses the *hook, line and sinker* approach to marketing.

Hook. To hook the target market, the advertiser uses various landmark words the target market can identify with. For instance, if the advertiser is targeting lumber companies, the headline may play on a phrase such as:

> You can't see the forest for the trees.

Add the word "now" and turn "can't" into "can" and you have:

> Now you can see the forest *and* the trees.

Or pose a question:

> Can you see the forest when looking at the trees?

Of course, the words forest and trees do not confine you to an audience of lumberjacks. See what happens if you add a subhead (below the headline) such as:

> Balance your books to the penny,
> and prepare your taxes in less than
> half the time it takes you now.

Suddenly you are talking to a small-business audience, one that keeps books and prepares its own taxes in-house.

Without a subhead, your readers have no idea what is being advertised—unless the headline is accompanied by an image that the target market can identify with or relate to on some level.

In business-to-consumer DRM, the job of the copywriter is to create desire and promise fulfillment. In business-to-business DRM, the job is to identify a problem and offer a solution.

As we will see, the incentive to act is actually part of the sinker. However, the incentive—or an allusion to an incentive—is often part of the hook:

> Now you can see the forest *and* the trees.
> Plus win a trip to the Rainforest!

Simply put, your goal with the hook is to hook the reader, to get the reader to continue to read. When you consider all the other ads out there, and the noise that interferes with this goal, you have to work very hard to accomplish your goal.

Line. The body copy, or line, reinforces how the product or service solves the problem, fills the need or satisfies the desire. It also builds trust by reassuring the client through guarantees, testimonials and the like. As well, it anticipates and overcomes any objections: People will not act if they have objections. In short, the body copy presents any other information the target market might need before they will take action, such as price, return policy and so on.

Sinker. This is the call to action. It tells readers what the advertiser wants them to do, how to do it, where to do it, and when to do it by.

The sinker generally uses a *time-limited incentive* to motivate the reader to buy the product, visit a website, call for a demo, make an appointment with a sale representative, fill out a survey that further qualifies the target market, and so forth.

Back to W5

To generate a response or close the sale, you have to motivate your target market to act. But you have to do more than offer an amazing incentive. You also have to tell your target market *everything they need to know* in order to respond to the ad.

What does the target market need to know?

Go back to the W5 questions (Chapter 4) and you will see many of the questions your target market is asking, consciously or subconsciously, as they read your DRM piece.

Let's review some of the W5 questions from the target market's point of view:

- Who is advertising?
- What is being advertised? (Product, service or cause)
- What are the features, assets and benefits associated with the product?
- What need/want/desire do I have for the product?
- What are the social/emotional/business benefits associated with the product?
- How do I feel after reading/hearing/viewing the ad?
- What guarantees do I have that the product will live up to the expectations generated by this ad?
- What action am I being asked to take (if any)?
- Why should I take it?

- What's in it for me?
- What incentive (if any) is being offered to induce action?
- When does the inducement to action expire?
- Where do I go to take action?
- When can/should I do it? How?

It is tough, almost impossible, to motivate your target market to take action without providing answers to those questions in a creative-yet-business-like manner that the target market can relate to. This is why direct response advertising typically uses more words than ads designed to build brand awareness.

The DRM Openings

When it comes to DRM, your hook is key. Successful direct response marketing focuses on the prospect, not the product. Before writing business-to-business DRM material, the most useful background research you can do is to ask your typical prospect: "What's the biggest problem you have right now?"

That can also be the case in business-to-consumer DRM, although you might want to focus on the greatest desire or aspiration of the target market. However, you can still think of it in terms of problem/solution: If the target market cannot achieve his/her desires and aspirations, the target market has a problem. And that, for the advertiser, provides an opportunity to offer a solution.

The hook should address or allude to that problem—and offer or allude to a solution. Some time-tested openings for DRM brochures or sales letters include:

- Ask a provocative question.
- Go straight to the heart of the reader's most pressing problem or concern.
- Arouse curiosity.
- Lead off with a fascinating fact or incredible statistic.
- State the offer up-front, especially if it involves money—saving it or receiving it. If you are offering something for an incredibly low price or making a free offer, say so.
- State the solution or problem up-front. If you are offering a solution to a problem, say so: "No more tangles!" Then outline the problem and state how your new hair conditioner solves it. Or start with a problem: "Tired of tangles?" Then detail the solution.

Below are some examples of DRM headlines that have produced solid results for advertisers.

An envelope teaser for a mailing that sold a manual on internal auditing procedures:

> 14 things that can go wrong in your company—
> and one sure way to prevent them

From a subscription letter for *Inc.* magazine:

> A special invitation to the hero of American business

An envelope teaser for a subscription mailing for *Financial World* magazine:

> Can 193,750 millionaires be wrong?

The lead paragraph of a fund-raising letter:

> Dear Friend: I'm fed up with the legal system. I want to change it and I think you do, too.

DRM Geography

In business-to-business DRM, the sales letter—not the outer envelope, the brochure or the reply form—is the most important part of the direct-mail package. However, you still need a powerful hook and an incentive, or at least an allusion to one, to get the reader to read the sales letter. (All things being equal, a DRM package with a letter will usually outperform a postcard, a brochure or an ad reprint mailed without a letter.)

Why do letters pull so well? A letter creates the illusion of personal communication. We are trained to view letters as *real* mail and brochures as *advertising*. Which is more important to you? A letter or an ad?

When it comes to getting the target market to open your DRM package, you need to know the *hot spots* or the geography of your direct-mail package. The hot spots are the spaces that get the most readership. Put your strongest selling copy in these spots:

- The front of the envelope
- The first paragraphs of the letter, its subheads, its last paragraph and the post-script (PS: 80% of readers look at the PS)
- The brochure cover, its subheads, and the headline of its inside spread
- Brochure picture captions
- The headline and copy on the order form or reply card

Magic Words

The magic words of DRM can dramatically increase response to your mailing. Often operating under the mistaken notion that the mission of the copywriter is to be creative, advertisers sometimes avoid the magic words of direct mail. They think the phrases are clichés. But clichés are familiar and people become engaged by the familiar. Just because a word or phrase is used frequently doesn't mean that it has lost its power to achieve your communications objective. In conversation, for example, "please" and "thank you" never go out of style.

What are the magic words of direct mail?

- *Free*. Are you giving away a brochure, report, consultation or gift? Say *free brochure*. Not *brochure*. Say *free consultation*. Not *initial consultation*. Say *free gift*. Not *gift*.

  If the English teacher in you objects that "free gift" is redundant, say: *Get thee behind me Mr. Conron*! A mail-order firm tested two packages. The only difference was that Package "A" offered a *gift* while Package "B" offered a *free gift*. Which ad did better? You guessed it. The free gift offered in Package "B" significantly out-pulled Package "A." What's more, many people who received Package "A" wrote in and asked whether the gift was free!

- *No obligation*. This is important when you are offering anything free. If prospects aren't obligated to use your firm's wastewater treatment services after you analyze their water sample for free, say so. People want to be reassured that there are no strings attached.

- *No salesperson will call*. If true, a fantastic phrase that can increase response rates. Most people, including genuine prospects, hate being called on by salespeople.

  Warning: Do not say "no salesperson will call" if you plan to follow up by phone. People won't buy from liars.

- *Details inside*. A line like that should follow any teaser copy on the outer envelope to direct the reader inside.

- *Limited time only*. People who put your mailing aside for later reading will probably never respond. The trick is to generate a response now. One way to do this is with a time-limited offer, either generic ("This offer is for a limited time only") or specific ("This offer expires 20/09/12").

- *Announcing* or *At last*. People like to think they are getting in on the ground floor of a new thing. Making your mailing an announcement increases its attention-getting powers.

- *New.* "New" is sheer magic in consumer mailings. But it's a double-edged sword in industrial mailings. On the one hand, business and technical buyers want something new. On the other hand, they demand products with proven performance. The solution? Explain that your product is new or available to them for the first time, but proven elsewhere—in another country, another application or another industry.

  For example, if you introduced a diagnostic display system, advertise it as "new" to US hospitals, but explain that it has been used successfully for five years in leading hospitals throughout Europe.

In the next chapter we look at the DRM sales letter, and then we will look at DRM in action. But first, what about DRM using email? Isn't DRM email just a fancy word for spam, spam, spam, spam, spam?

What About Direct Response Email Marketing?

Direct response email marketing is less costly than printed DRM material that is mailed to the target market. Long considered a lightweight in the advertising world and often confused with spam, email marketing has come a long way. However, it has a long way to go to reach the magnitude of the traditional DRM industry. The billion dollars (and growing) spent on email marketing in 2010 may seem paltry in comparison with the $200-billion direct mail market, but email is gathering momentum while direct mail seems to have peaked.

The reason? Primarily cost. Email campaigns cost $5 to $7 per thousand, compared with the $500 to $750 (or more) per thousand for direct mail. As well, they are quicker to execute, they get faster results and their success (or failure) can be measured more easily (by click-throughs and sales the day the email lands).

Email marketing is not spam, if used on an opt-in or permission basis. However, there are risks to sending DRM email. Email users are so overwhelmed by spam these days they use a number of filtering techniques to keep it out of their in-boxes, so DRM email may be caught in spam filters. Occasionally, email users forget they granted permission for a marketer to send them email and they may view the DRM email as spam.

The challenge for email marketers is to make the message so relevant to the person receiving it that it is not confused with spam. And the offer must be compelling enough to make the recipient act on it.

Email marketers should:

- Use strong, provocative or self-explanatory subjects lines
- Keep the message to one computer screen (page)
- Include a link to a website for more information
- Include an incentive to click on the link
- Include unsubscribe information
- Ensure those who unsubscribe get off the list

Chapter 16: Direct Response Sales Letter

As the name implies, sales letters are used to sell something to someone. In order to sell anyone anything, you have to persuade him or her to take action—to buy. However, if you are selling an expensive (and possibly complex) product or service—an IT solution, a backhoe for commercial construction use, accounting and auditing services—the action you desire might not be "buy" even though you are writing a sales letter, because people don't purchase expensive and complex products off the shelf the way they buy DVDs, books or socks.

You might, instead, want the reader to take a pre-purchase action—call for more information, visit your website, arrange for a sales representative to call, and so on. In short, before you write a sales letter or any copy meant to persuade, you need to know what action you are trying to persuade the reader to take. If you don't know your purpose and the action you want to reader to take, how can you achieve your purpose and motivate the reader to take a particular action?

As I have said previously, anytime you want anyone to do something—even attend a meeting—you are "selling" and you have to motivate the person to act or respond (*buy* into what you want, so to speak). Knowing what you want the reader to do, and motivating the reader to do it, is at the heart of any persuasive message—such as advertising copy and direct response marketing copy—and the focus of this chapter on sales letters and proposal cover letters.

The typical sales letter does the following:

- Lets the reader know your purpose—why you are writing
- Introduces you to the reader and makes a connection between you (your company, your products and/or your services, or your proposal) and the reader's problem, issue or opportunity
- Demonstrates that you understand the client's objectives and, depending on the circumstance, the client's target market and how what you are selling or proposing relates to the client's objectives and/or target market
- Extols the virtues of your company, products and/or services, or summarizes (and extols the virtues of) your proposal
- Calls for a defined action; motivates the reader to act

Three-section Sales Letter

Sales letters and proposal cover letters should be divided into three sections:

Introduction

- Hooks the reader (captures attention) with a line that relates to a problem, issue, opportunity or situation the reader is familiar with or can relate to
- Continues to hold the reader's interest by proposing a solution, alternative, or means of exploiting the opportunity
- Makes clear the purpose of the letter

Body

- Continues to hold interest; starts to influence attitude
- May overcome anticipated objections (major attitude adjustment technique)
- May include rationale for and/or benefits of proposal
- May include schedule (timelines) and a detailed projection of costs (proposed budget)

Conclusion

- Calls for action and outlines next steps and how to take them; details who proposes to do what for whom, when, where and why
- May offer an incentive to motivate the reader to act
- Demonstrates willingness to answer questions or provide more details

You might use attention-grabbing subheadings that create distinct sections in a sales letter, but you do not have to. Either way, you should be aware that the role of each section, as described above, is distinct. Even so, you need to write so that there are logical transitions between sections and a logical flow from section to section.

Cold-call Sales Letter Example

Let's look at a cold-call sales letter. Also known as an unsolicited sales letter or direct response marketing letter, a cold-call sales letter is a letter you send to someone who has not requested it. Some people term unsolicited letters "junk mail." Such letters might feel like junk mail to consumers who are bombarded with unsolicited credit card applications and sales flyers; however, cold-call sales letters are a staple of business-to-business communication. They are often used to make initial contact with a prospect or to generate leads for a company's sales force, as in the sales letter example below.

Note: As mentioned, if you send your sales letter by email, and you do not have permission to email a business or consumer, it will be considered spam and will most likely be deleted, no matter how legitimate your business is. Building email lists and using permission-based email marketing go beyond the scope of this book; however, if you are planning an email marketing campaign, make sure you investigate how to properly build permission-based email lists.

Dear Ms. Bussman:

Are you having trouble keeping your cool? When you turn on the air conditioning, do you feel as if you are wasting energy and money? PLR Air Conditioning would like to demonstrate how we can help you keep cool and save energy too—all for less than you might have imagined.

We would like to demonstrate how the installation of a PLR air-conditioning system will keep your plant and office cool and reduce energy costs. The demonstration takes 45 minutes, and it will not disrupt your business operations.

We believe that you will find PLR systems to be practical, efficient and economical.

PLR has been in the industrial heating and air-conditioning business for over 40 years, servicing companies like yours. We are a member of the Better Business Bureau and have a stellar credit rating. You can view our client list and read a number of testimonials on our website, www.plr.com.

Please review the information in the enclosed brochure and call us for a demonstration. What do you have to lose? Certainly not your cool! To set up a demonstration, call 416-555-5555.

If you call us by May 31, we will conduct a free energy efficiency audit and show you 10 no-cost ways to cut your company's electricity bill.

Sincerely,
James P. Callahan
Sales Manager

Components of a Cold-call Sales Letter

Now, let's examine the component parts of the sales letter.

Introduction: The letter starts with humour (risky, I confess) to capture the attention of (hook) the reader. Notice how the word "cool" used in the introduction is related to the product, and how quickly the writer connects the opening line to the product—connects cool to air conditioning. By the third sentence, the reader knows exactly why the writer is writing (purpose)—to conduct a demonstration. Notice how the purpose is supported by a benefit statement implying cost savings. In other words, the writer is supporting his purpose by letting the reader know that PLR can solve a problem.

> Are you having trouble keeping your cool? When you turn on the air conditioning, do you feel as if you are wasting energy and money? PLR Air Conditioning would like to demonstrate how we can help keep you cool and save energy too—all for less than you might have imagined.

Body: Once the purpose is established, the body expands on it while maintaining interest and influencing attitude. The body overcomes a possible objection: This will probably take all day. No, it "takes 45 minutes." It also focuses on information that is of interest to the client by promising to "reduce the cost of energy," and to be "practical, efficient, economical."

> We would like to demonstrate how the installation of a PLR air-conditioning system will keep your plant and office cool and reduce the cost of energy. The demonstration takes 45 minutes, and it will not disrupt your business operations.

> We believe that you will find PLR systems to be practical, efficient and economical.

The company also uses the body to build trust, just in case the reader is wondering who the heck PLR is.

> PLR has been in business for over 40 years, servicing companies like yours. We are a member of the Better Business Bureau and have a stellar credit rating. You can view our client list and read a number of testimonials on our website, www.plr.com.

Conclusion: Here the letter asks the reader to do something—read a brochure and make a call. The writer would be happy if the reader just called, but if the reader is interested, but not quite convinced, she can review additional information in the brochure. The conclusion succinctly summarizes what the letter has been about and echoes the opening, as if reminding the reader what caught her attention in the first place:

> What do you have to lose? Certainly not your cool!

The conclusion also offers the reader a limited-time incentive to act. Within ten days, PLR will know how effective its cold-call sales letter was. If the company sends out two hundred letters and has 10 or 20 replies, the letter would be considered a direct mail success. With that in mind, if you are ever conducting a direct mail campaign, sample your audience first. Say you want to send out two thousand letters. Send out a hundred letters first and gauge the response. If you come up empty, you will want to review and revise your sales message.

Follow-up Sales Letter

In the post-demonstration follow-up sales letter, the same principles apply. The writer does not have to work as hard at hooking the reader but the writer must still capture the reader's attention. Analyze this letter to see how its structure adheres to the introduction, body and conclusion methodology of writing persuasive cold-call sales letters.

Dear Ms. Bussman:

We hope you were able to see how a PLR air-conditioning system would provide energy efficiency, cool comfort, and the maximum return on your investment when we demonstrated the system for you on October 30.

We would like to thank Mr. Lindsay and Mrs. Smooth from your operations division for joining us for the demonstration.

As discussed, the equipment PLR proposes to install is modular in design, so you can add additional units as the need arises. This makes it practical, efficient and economical, both now and in the future. Therefore, the system protects you against obsolescence as your business continues to grow.

I will follow up on the attached proposal on November 11. The information it provides should answer any pricing and timing questions you might have. However, if you require additional information before November 11, please call me.

In addition, I have attached your free energy efficiency audit results showing you 10 no-cost ways to cut your energy bill.

Sincerely,
James P. Callahan
Sales Manager

Proposal Cover Letter

If your company issues proposals, perhaps in response to a request for quote (RFQ) or a request for proposal (RFP), you should write a proposal cover letter. The sales letter principles apply to proposal cover letters; however, the action you want the reader to take is to read your proposal, not call or buy—at least not until they've read the proposal. The proposal itself will call for a specific action.

Think of your proposal cover letter as you would an executive summary of a report (which we will look at later in the book). Your cover letter is your opportunity to summarize your proposal in a way that motivates the letter reader to read your proposal.

Using the introduction/body/conclusion format, your proposal cover letter (or cover email if you have permission to email your proposal, perhaps as a PDF file) should tell the reader that there is something they need to know in the proposal accompanying your letter or in the attached file.

Many companies write skimpy proposal cover letters or do not include cover letters with proposals. I am not going to say that their proposals will never be read; however, there may be times when a busy executive shoves such proposals to the bottom of the pile or simply bypasses them.

In other words, imagine if you had a stack of proposals in front of you, and a limited time to read them. You would glance briefly at the cover letters and separate the proposals that were of interest from those that were not, based on the cover letter. In short, a well-structured, well-written proposal cover letter can motivate the reader to read your proposal.

Let's look at a proposal cover letter (below) set up in full-block style. The letter is based on the CAGA Ambrosia apple case study. The CAGA wants to hold a fall fair in New York and Central PR is submitting a bid to manage and promote the event.

Direct Response Sales Letter

Central PR

123 Any Street, Toronto, Ontario M6R 1K7

416.555.1212 - pr@centralpr.com

June 3, 2008

Mr. Johnny McDonald
President
Canadian Apple Growers Association
123 McIntosh Boulevard
Milton, Ontario, L6T 1X4

Dear Mr. McDonald:

Take a bite out of the Big Apple—Ambrosia Style!

That is what Central PR proposes to help the Canadian Apple Growers Association do as we promote the exciting New York City unveiling of the Ambrosia apple. Central PR will promote your Canadian-style Fall Fair in Central Park and manage the event for you.

For one low price, as outlined in the enclosed proposal, we will:

- Write and issue the media release to promote the Fair
- Compile an accurate list of media attendees
- Create the media kit
- Welcome media at the event; arrange interviews with reporters
- Track all media hits connected with your event
- Calculate the media exposure value for the CAGA

You want this event to be as unblemished as the Ambrosia, and Central PR is the agency to ensure the PR for the Fall Fair runs smoothly. Central PR has been in the public relations business since 1999. We have successfully staged media events in Toronto, Montreal, Vancouver, Los Angeles and New York City. From fashion to fruit, we have the experience to promote your association.

The enclosed proposal details the program of events and publicity agenda we are proposing for the Canadian-style Fall Fair. In addition, it includes suggested dates for the event, timelines that will enable you to successfully promote and stage the event, a list of the duties and responsibilities that Central PR will cover on your behalf, a full budget, bios of our executive team and testimonials.

After you read our Fall Fair proposal, feel free to call me with any questions you may have or to schedule a meeting. We hope to meet by the end of May to discuss this exciting opportunity to represent the CAGA, as the Ambrosia apple makes its New York debut.

Sincerely,

Nadine Leclair
Marketing Manager
Central PR

As the reader, do you feel Central PR understands your promotional objective? Do you feel the PR agency possesses the ability to help you organize and promote an event that will help you achieve your objective? If so, you will read the proposal. If the proposal is sound, and the price is right, you will call and set up a meeting.

"Sale" achieved, even though you have not yet bought anything.

You would not, in fact, buy this PR service without a meeting. If Central PR is not able to sell you on the concept of the initial meeting, it cannot close the actual sale. In other words, sometimes you have to achieve a preliminary purpose before you can achieve your ultimate purpose. Keep that in mind when you are writing a sales letter or any document.

Sales Letter Exercise

See if you can put the sales letter writing principles into effect by writing a sales letter or proposal cover letter.

If you don't have anything to write about, but want to try this exercise, produce a sales letter or proposal cover letter based on the Chez Restaurant case study below.

As with the letter above, pretend that you are a public relations firm responding to a request for proposal to stage the event outlined in the case study. Or you might pretend that you are a PR firm that is seeking new business. Part of your business plan calls for you to develop and pitch PR ideas to companies that have upcoming events—such as the launch of the Ambrosia apple or the opening of Chez Restaurant.

In other words, you can pretend that you have not been asked to submit a proposal but that you are writing a cold-call sales letter meant to solicit PR work from CAGA or Chez Restaurant.

Either way, your letter should capture the reader's attention, hold his or her interest, influence the reader's attitude and cause the reader to take a specific action. Do this with a sales letter that has three distinct sections—introduction, body and conclusion—and smooth transitions between each section.

Before you start, ask yourself a couple of questions:

- *What's in it for the reader?* Your letter should answer that.

- *What is the action that I am trying to motivate?* Your letter should build to asking for the order or the action you want to take place.

Chez Restaurant Case Study

Henri Blanc has hired your public relations agency to promote an event in Toronto to attract media attention and to create awareness about his new upscale French bistro in Yorkville, Chez Restaurant.

Background information: There are more restaurants per capita in the City of Toronto than in almost any other city in North America; competition among high-end restaurants is fierce. Chez Restaurant has a prime location, valet parking, and a Cordon Bleu chef, Michel Boeuf. He was trained in Paris, France, where he worked for 20 years in five-star restaurants.

Your menu is world class, as is your décor. Your prices reflect your chef, menu, and the dining experience, which is private, personal and exquisite. You expect to attract celebrities, CEOs and deal-makers.

The idea: To invite selected media—business editors and restaurant reviewers—to a grand opening gala party featuring fine finger foods and wine tasting. Jazz singer and crooner Michael Bublé would provide the entertainment. The event would include brief presentations by Blanc and Boeuf. The gala will be held the day before the opening of the Toronto International Film Festival; a number of movie stars, producers, and directors have accepted invitations to the opening.

The invited media and guests will receive private invitations. This release announces the grand opening gala, complete with red carpet. The goal is to create buzz with a big splash outside the restaurant—fans and media lining the red carpet; lots of red carpet photo opportunities—while providing guests with an intimate and private experience inside the restaurant.

Your task: Reply to a request for proposal seeking an agency to stage this event or send a cold-call sales letter pitching your PR agency as an agency that could stage a grand-opening event.

Chapter 17: DRM in Action

When the TV show, *Survivor*, became a hit, Rogers, a Canadian cable TV company, sent a direct response marketing (DRM) brochure to homes in areas where Rogers offers cable service. Allow me to qualify that: They sent it to homes *without* cable in areas where Rogers offers cable service. (Why would the company send an expensive, full-colour brochure to existing Rogers cable clients?)

The brochure used the following headline:

Why Survive without Cable?
Get connected and join the cast today.

When the reader opened the brochure, they were greeted with a pop-up incentive:

Order Rogers Cable service before March 15, 2003
and your installation is FREE.
PLUS! Enjoy your first two months at 1/2 price!

Of course, the call to action immediately followed:

To order, call < number>... Or order online at <website>.

It was a timely and topical pitch with a solid incentive meant to motivate action, and it was aimed directly at Rogers's target market—those without cable. Notice how the ad's graphics support the copy. Or, in short, how the copy and graphics support the concept that might be summed up as: To survive (be fulfilled, live a full life), you need cable.

Accept or reject the concept, that's your choice as a consumer. But appreciate how the graphics and words work together to make the concept real, and how the direct response mailing is sent to those most likely to buy—consumers without cable who live in the areas served by Rogers.

If you are not into heavy-duty construction equipment, the next DRM headline will not appeal to you. Why should it? You are not the target market. However, if you are a heavy-duty construction kind of person, you will dig it, so to speak.

MEET THE BACKHOE LOADER
YOU'LL BE PROUD TO HAVE ON YOUR STAFF.

This headline personifies the product, turning it into a hard-working member of the staff. This product is someone, rather than something, you would be proud to have on your team. Just so you know, the image that accompanies the headline shows the backhoe working hard at a construction site. However, a picture and related headline may not be enough to entice the reader to open the brochure. So what does Volvo, the backhoe manufacturer, offer, right on the front page of the DRM piece?

LOOK INSIDE FOR YOUR CHANCE
TO WIN A CRUISE FROM VOLVO!

In short, Volvo offers an incentive to get readers to open the direct mail brochure. How do readers qualify for a chance to win a cruise? As you will see, the incentive is tied directly with Volvo's call to action—schedule a demonstration—or what the company wants the reader to do.

A backhoe is an expensive product or a complex sale. People don't just call up and say, "I'll take two, please." Volvo knows that closing the sale takes personal contact. So the call to action is not "Buy now!" The call to action is: *Schedule a demonstration*. Readers can do this online or by fax, "and be entered into the Choose Your Cruise Contest."

To ensure readers act sooner rather than later, the incentive is followed by an expiry date. The offer expires about a month after the date the flyer was mailed.

What does the advertiser know in four weeks? In four weeks, Volvo will have feedback. The company knows how many brochures were mailed and it will know how many demonstrations were scheduled. If the company is wise, it will track sales based on demonstrations scheduled as a result of this mailing. In short, based on feedback motivated by an incentive, Volvo will be able to determine if the direct response mailing was successful. Or not. If it was, they can repeat similar offers. If not, they can go back to the drawing-board and revamp the DRM piece.

Take a look at this DRM copy from RBC Insurance, and automotive insurance company. On the front of the DRM brochure, mailed to consumers with cars, is this simple headline:

RBC insurance shrinks the *KRUNCH* of auto accidents.

There is no sinker or incentive, but there is a savings involved in "shrinks the krunch." In addition, if, like most people, you turn the brochure over before you open it, you see the following:

FREE $25 gas gift card when you complete an auto insurance quote.
- ➢ In person – at an RBC branch
- ➢ By phone – 1-800-xxx-xxxx

So there is a savings on the cover, meant to motivate you to read, and a sinker or incentive, one that the target market—car owners—can related to, prominently displayed on the back, meant to motivate you to act. And notice that the action is not "buy" insurance. The purpose of the brochure is to get readers to come in or call for a quote. Do that, you get a free gas card.

The company must feel that its rates are competitive enough that it will close enough quotes to cover the cost of the gas cards. Or that it will keep enough of the customers it obtains from this promotion for long enough to more than cover the cost of the gas cards. In short, if the cost of the company's promotion was so exorbitant that it could not be recouped from the people who acted on the offer, it would not make business sense. So the incentive is important; profiting from it is too.

Let's take a look at another DRM brochure. On the cover we have the following:

Your FREE month is waiting for you!

That's all it says. Full stop. As the consumer receiving this, you have no idea from that line (there is no graphic on the cover) what product or service is being promoted. The question is: Are you motivated by this incentive to take a look. I'd suggest that most people would at least take a quick look. If the product or service was something they were interested in, they'd read on.

Of course, the call to action for the phone and Internet service (gee, are you surprised?) includes a reminder of the incentive on the cover that motivated you to look:

Sign up today and receive one month FREE!

Oh, and in case you have that typical objective that most consumers have when they see an offer like this—"I bet I have to lock into a long-term contract to get the free month"—there is an short, direct, attitude-adjusting line that overcomes that fully anticipated objective:

Contract-free!

So, as you have seen, there are many ways to motivate a reader to read and too act. But they all involve some sense of an attention-grabbing hook and incentive, a hook that implies an incentive, or an incentive that hooks you.

Remember Poetry?

The Volvo DRM body copy begins by reinforcing the *proud staff member* concept established by the headline:

> The hardest-working employee wasn't always the impressive piece of machinery it is today.

In the next line, you can almost hear the copywriting shift gears. *Now that I have your attention, let me write something that will hold your interest*:

> Our engineers thought big when designing our backhoe loaders. The loader has the strength and simplicity of a Volvo Wheel Loader. The backhoe has the power and performance of a Volvo Excavator. All with an operator's station that will envelop you in comfort and serviceability features that will ensure a long productive life.

If none of that means anything to you, don't worry. All that means is that you are not Volvo's target market. Remember, to be effective, the copy must speak to the target market, which is why the copywriter needs to know what the target market knows and does not know (thinks and does not think, feels and does not feel) about the product.

Who Aspires to This?

Earlier in the book, I mentioned that advertisers often show images that reflect their target market's desires or how the target market aspires to be perceived.

Now think about poetry, how opposites belong in the same set. For instance, black and white belong together, as do hot and cold, or civilized and rugged.

Keep that in mind and you will understand the image in the Staples direct mail flyer.

Who aspires to be this fellow (below)? Dare I say, *Nobody*!

Notice how the illustration and the headline/subhead of this Staples DRM piece work together. If you have ever felt disorganized (disorganization is a business problem), then Staples has a solution.

The image represents the disorganized feeling. The first word in the headline (*Note...*) plays on the Post-It Notes in the image. The headline also uses the word *organized*, which is the complete opposite of how the chap in the image, covered in Post-It Notes, looks. So there we have our poetry.

While the man in the ad looks disorganized, he represents how many small-business owners feel. He does not represent what they aspire to; he represents how they feel. Remember that opposites are the same (thematically), so he represents how they do not want to feel as well.

Besides, once this business owner acts on this DRM offer and shops at Staples, he will no longer look and feel this way. Isn't that what the ad is promising? The question is: How do we get the reader to act?

When you turn the Staples direct mail flyer over, you see a time-limited incentive meant to inspire the reader to spend a minimum of $200:

> Save $30
> Off your next purchase of $200 or more
> Mention or enter coupon code 75402 when placing your order....

This copy is, of course, followed by an expiry date in small print. The offer expires about two weeks from the date the flyer was mailed. So in two weeks, Staples will know if the DRM mailing was successful. Or not.

If so, they can repeat similar offers. If not, they can go back to the drawing-board.

Now notice how hard this left-leaning magazine is working to get DRM recipients to open the envelope and read more. Analyze the copy carefully and you will see all the elements there—hook, line and sinker—on the front of the envelope.

Then, once you get inside, the elements are repeated in a sales letter, one that pays more attention to the line, but still uses a hook to capture attention all over again, and repeats the sinker—the incentive that pushed you over the edge and got you to open the darn envelope in the first place.

This is the front of the envelope:

The magazine purchased the subscription list of another left-leaning magazine, so they are speaking to their target market. However, instead of congratulating their potential readers on being progressive, they are challenging them and challenging their complacency.

Get uncomfortable.
Experience for yourself the new magazine that is
informing, challenging, entertaining, and shaking up
Canada—and Canadians—like never before.
START WITH A FREE COPY OF THE NEXT ISSUE!

Notice how the headline (hook) and the subhead or envelope body copy (line) address the reader directly using second person: *you* (understood in the command or imperative statement used in the headline) and *yourself.* Notice how the subhead carries through with the uncomfortable theme established in the headline: *shaking up.* In addition, like a wise direct-marketing capitalist, the advertiser use that time-tested and proven DRM tool, the incentive (sinker):

Start with a FREE COPY of the next issue!

What is this magazine? You will have to open the envelope to find out! But we can presume it leans left of centre in scope, even though it is using very traditional marketing techniques to sell subscriptions. And why wouldn't it? After all, the techniques work!

DRM Body Copy

DRM letters and brochures tend to be copy heavy, but they are also designed for easy reading. They have to provide the reader with all the information the reader needs to take action, but they must also look like they are easy, not a chore, to read. With that in mind, let's look at how some DRM body copy presented information while building on the headline.

Here is a headline from a Grocery Gateway direct mail piece:

> Let us deliver your groceries
> And we'll save you $20

Through a solution, the headline alludes to a problem: Who has time to shop? The solution is to let Grocery Gateway deliver. And, of course, the incentive is front and centre.

Open the brochure and what do you see?

> You have more important things to do than go grocery shopping.
> We don't.

The copy immediately picks up on the *theme* established by the headline on the cover of the brochure.

The copy continues:

> We're GroceryGateway.com. We're committed to helping you simplify your life by taking away one weekly chore—your grocery shopping. We know you've got more important things to do with your time. Let us fill the pantry and fridge for you. We carefully select, pack and deliver your whole shopping list right to your door (or even your kitchen counter if that's where you'd like it).

Notice how the theme continues with "simplify your life" and "taking away one weekly chore." Also, though, notice how the copy is already building trust and anticipating and overcoming objections. In case you think nobody will treat your groceries as well as you do, the copy informs you that "We carefully select, pack and deliver...."

One of the major objections to shopping online for groceries concerns the quality of produce and meat—products shoppers like to see before they buy. If the copy did not address that objection, it could not close the sale.

How does the copy address the objection? It poses the question that's on the mind of the reader and then answers it. Notice how the writer has fun with the answer and how that fun places particular emphasis on the answer while causing the reader to smile (to become engaged in the copy):

Fresh produce and meat online?

We're particularly picky about our perishables. We know you demand the freshest food and highest quality for your family. All our fruits, vegetables and meats are expertly sourced by industry professionals and kept in our Market Centre at their optimal temperature for freshness. After all, a bruised tomato will bruise our reputation.

The copy goes on to describe how the prices are competitive with the average grocery store in Toronto (this was mailed in Toronto), how there are weekly specials, what the minimum order is, what delivery fee is charged, and acceptable methods of payment—including credit cards accepted. In other words, this is just like shopping at a store; there are no inconveniences to shopping online. Objection overcome. And you don't have to travel. Advantage delivered.

If you still have doubt, there is the *promise*:

Our Promise

We are here to make your life simple, not more complicated. If something isn't right with your order, we'll fix it. Guaranteed. We stand behind our service, our people and our products with a 100% satisfaction guarantee. Go on. Let us help. What do you have to lose, except one more chore?

Notice how "guaranteed" is a one-word sentence. For emphasis. And how the copy concludes with a reference that takes you back to the beginning—in case you forgot how you got hooked and why you are actually reading a piece of so-called junk mail. Much like poetry, it comes full circle!

You shop online.

We deliver.

Now this is progress.

There is more information describing how easy it is to shop online. Plus there is an email address and phone number for those who may have questions. And it ends with a slogan.

Of course, there is a code to enter when shopping online to save $20, and an expiry date on the offer to motivate readers to act and act now!

Writing DRM Copy

Remember the seven items for which you wrote copy? Now it's time to review the work and convert ad copy into hook, line and sinker DRM copy. By way of review, you wrote copy for: *WriteOn!, CrashFree PC, Taxing Incentives, Full in Five, Ch0c0late, Magnetique* and *You.*

Review what you wrote. What was your purpose? If you are writing DRM copy, what should your purpose be? Remember, it doesn't have to be to sell. But it can be. Your purpose will change, based on the nature of the product and how complex it is to sell the product. You might want a consumer to buy. You might want your prospect to ask for more information, or perhaps ask to have a sales representative call.

For instance, if you are selling *you* to a prospective employer, you might want the action to be an interview—even though your ultimate goal is to land a job. You can't get the job without the interview, so your purpose is to set that up. In short, you define the action and make it happen.

Before You Begin, Ask....

- Whom am I going to sell to?
- How do I get the reader to open the envelope, flip open the brochure or open the email?
- What objections might I meet? What do I say to overcome them?
- What is required to build trust?
- What action do I want the reader to take?
- How do I motivate action (within a given period of time)? What incentive do I use to motivate action?

Rewrite Your Copy

With those questions in mind, rewrite your copy. Write the hook, line and sinker. But first, establish a concept that speaks to your target market. Pose a question that is most likely on the mind (or just below the surface) of the target market. Or raise a problem (without using negative language) and position your product or service as a solution. Or create a desire and position your product as that which fulfills the desire.

If appropriate, make your incentive part of the hook. But make sure you detail it or reinforce it when issuing your call to action (writing your sinker). Before you get to your call to action, build trust. Offer proof that your product does that which you claim it does. Detail appropriate features and benefits. Reassure the prospective client with guarantees, testimonials and the like, and overcome any anticipated objections.

If that seems like a large task, return to the Writing Process (Chapter 5). Before you begin to write, outline the points you will cover in the order you think you should cover them. Once you have your outline, you can move the order around until you think it all makes logical sense. *Then begin to write your copy.*

Or apply what you have learned to products and services that you are promoting.

Chapter 18: Brochure Writing Process

Remember VCVC? It's time to revisit the soda pop. This time you are going to create a brochure to encourage convenience store owners to stock VCVC. Why would we do this? If we can't get the product in stores, how are we going to sell it?

With that in mind, let's look at our goal(s) and at VCVC from the convenience store's perspective:

- **Define your sales/marketing objective or purpose:**
  Educate retailer about VCVC and motivate retailer to stock the pop.

- **Define/describe target market:**
  Convenience store owner; runs small business; conservative in nature but wants traffic from paying customers with money no matter what their outlook/attitude.

- **Target market's objections:**
  Store shelf space is at a premium; sees inventory as money tied up; wants products that draw crowds and move off the shelves.

- **Overcome objections:**
  Ad campaign will create awareness; phase 2 of campaign, coupons will motivate consumers to buy; budget price and unique taste will keep them coming back. Convenient case of six-pack cans; grab-and-go 16 oz. plastic bottles; easy to stock and store; high-volume and high-margin product. (Anything else you can offer to overcome the fear, i.e. objection, the retailer might have about getting stuck with stock if sales fall flat?)

- **Build trust:**
  VCVC Inc. is a well-financed, privately held company. VCVC is first of three brands slated for rollout over the next year, focusing on urban market in Canada. Manufacturing facilities in Toronto, Montreal, Edmonton and Calgary; 48-hour distribution fulfillment guaranteed. Company produces in-store brands for several major supermarkets; ISO 9000 certified. Guaranteed pick-up of overstock in first three months.

- **Call to action:**
  Call, fax or email the sales department and place order; visit website and order online in secure environment. Offer discount incentive to motivate order, particularly online orders. (Why might a company try to motivate online orders?)

- **Incentive:**
  Ideally, create your own. You can use a 15% discount off the wholesale price on initial orders, minimum 12 cases of four-pack cans or six cases of bottles (12 bottles to a case). Or buy 12 cases of cans or bottles and receive one free case. Order must be placed by June 25 (three weeks after DRM piece arrives). Why then? The VCVC consumer ads hit shortly after that because VCVC wants to gear up for Canada Day and summer sales. But feel free to come up with creative incentives that appeal to this particular target market.

Writing Brochure Copy

Before you start to write your copy:

- Create a **concept** you can hang your copy on.

- Find/explore **landmark words** and phrases your target market identifies with and that you can associate with your concept and/or product.

- **Brainstorm/Cluster**: *Convenience store*. As you are clustering: Think small-business owners. Think customers. Think VCVC. Ultimately, you must demonstrate how VCVC fulfills the target market's need to satisfy customers *and* move product.

- **Revisit your concept and come up with your hook**: Based on your concept, what is your hook, your attention-grabbing headline the target market can identify with? Also, think of your image and make sure the headline and image connect with each other.
  - o In a creative and positive manner, your hook should define, or at least allude to, the problem that VCVC is going to solve, or the benefits it will bring. And you should hint at or spell out your incentive, perhaps in the subhead or copy below the subhead, but definitely on the first page.

- **Write your line(s)**: Demonstrate knowledge of your target market's business needs/problems and offer an immediate solution. Build trust in your company, product and offer. Perhaps you might even want to give the retailer a taste of the consumer marketing campaign that will drive traffic to the store. Also, the retailer may not be aware of VCVC, so make sure you describe your product, perhaps even position it against the competition.

- **Sinker**: Close the sale with your incentive and a call to action tied to your incentive. Don't forget to motivate the reader to act sooner rather than later! And don't forget to let the reader know how to act, what steps to take to order from you.

But We're a Charity!

I often get the "we're a charity" objection to DRM. First off, see how the left-leaning magazine used basic DRM principles. The process—no matter what you are promoting—is the same.

Even if you are promoting a charitable or political cause, *the process is the same*. You still need to capture attention, hold interest, influence attitude, issue a call to action and motivate action. If you are a charity, you might not offer me a vacation or a discount to motivate me to act, but your incentive should be there and it should be appropriate to who you are, who your target market is, and what you action you want your target market to take.

I've had some non-profit organizations tell me that they have no incentives to offer. Again, it may very well be the case that you cannot give a discount on a donation, or guarantee the person will feel good if they donate twice as much as they did last time. Or can you? Ultimately, there are things you can do. It's up to you to think creatively and to come up with an appropriate sinker.

What is it the donor wants or desires? While some people might donate out of a principled sense of obligation, many people want to be recognized or acknowledged. Others want to know that their contribution is making a difference, perhaps a particular kind of difference. Try to get into the heads of your donors and find out what they want, and then build an incentive that motivates them to act.

Here are *a few for instances*, but don't stop thinking. You have to do what works best for you. For instance, you might:

- Include their name on an honour or donor roll in your next mailing, or on your website, or on a donor's wall where you do your charitable business; create levels that correspond with donations of various amounts.

- Send them a certificate of donation, a decal, or even mailing labels that they can display.

- Work with corporate sponsors to offer donors free CDs or DVDs, or discounts on products/services.
- Let them know they will receive letters from people their donation has helped, or receive a monthly newsletter outlining progress on whatever project they are supporting.

Rest assured, there are many more incentives that you can offer them. Think like your target market; or better yet, survey people who have supported your cause in the past. Find out what they need to know, hear and/or would like to receive to continue to do so.

Chapter 19: Web-based DRM

When it comes to direct response marketing (DRM) and the web, all the rules apply—more or less. What's cool about the web is that prospects often find you using Google or other search engines. They enter keywords related to your product or service, and up pops a link to your website or an ad on Google, Yahoo! or Bing.

The searcher, who has pre-qualified himself or herself by entering keywords related to your product, service or cause, clicks on the link and lands on your home page or any other page you have optimized (see Chapter 20) to show up in a search engine, based on specific search terms.

If the searcher clicks on a Google ad—known as AdWords—the ad should take the prospect to what is known as a *landing page*—your online DRM page—not to your home page.

What is the difference between a home page and a landing page? A home page has a web address such as www.yoursite.com and generally includes links to all the main pages on a website. A landing page might have a web address such as www.yoursite.com/product-info and is set up to solicit a direct response from a prospect that lands on it after clicking on a link or an online ad.

Landing Page: A web page that users click to from an online ad. Landing pages are used by advertisers who wish to provide a special offer in response to a click-through on a banner ad or pay-per-click (PPC) ad. For best results, these pages are highly targeted to the person who might click on the ad, and are set up using DRM principles.

While the landing page does not have to include all the elements that a DRM brochure requires, a landing page and pages it links to can offer much more information than DRM brochures because a landing page offers the *hotlink advantage*. In other words, instead of including every detail required to close the sale on the landing page, the hotlink advantage lets you incorporate links on your landing page that visitors can click on for more information. For instance, you can create a link from the landing page to a full list of features and benefits, or to the complete details of your guarantee.

Having said that, some advertisers believe you should put everything you want to say about your product or service on the landing page itself, rather than linking to other pages. That tends to work best in business-to-consumer marketing. In business-to-business marketing, you can use hotlinks to your advantages, turning your landing page into a micro website that closes the sale.

Whether you include all the copy required to close the sale on the landing page (as some DRM landing pages do) or on the landing page and on various hot-linked pages, you still need a hook, line and sinker. However, the first thing you need is a call to action, perhaps in conjunction with a sinker (incentive to act). Think about it. The visitor to your landing page is a hot prospect. He or she pre-qualified by using keywords related to your product *and* clicked on a Google ad or search engine link about your product. Why wouldn't you offer the visitor a way to buy—a link that says "Buy Now!" or at least "Try Now!" (if you are selling software, for instance)? If the visitor is a hot prospect, he can buy. If she is just curious, she can continue to read your landing page copy.

Busy as a Bee

Below is the landing page for U-Rent-It Manager (URIM), a party/event rental and small equipment rental order-entry and reservation software system. (The application is real; the name has been changed.)

If you have ever rented equipment or tools, you probably feel lucky if the reserved equipment is there when you show up. The equipment rental staff are running around like chickens with their heads cut off and you wonder if they actually know what they are doing. These folks are busy, no doubt about it. But are they organized?

The U-Rent-It Manager application claims it will organize inventory and staff so that rental customers get the products they have reserved. URIM has a Google AdWords campaign. The ads take the prospect to the URIM landing page, where the first thing visitors see is a link to a 30-day free trial offer for the application. Click on the link and you see guarantees and other trust-building copy, as well as a link to the terms and conditions (kept as simple as possible) and, of course, the download link.

The sales offer is put up front because visitors have prequalified themselves by using keywords to search for such a product and just might want to buy it. So why not make it easy to buy, or at least try? (Layout and design are important to make the page easy to read and the requested action easy to follow.)

But what if the visitor still needs convincing? The landing page contains sales and promotional copy as well. Notice the use of bullet points in the sample copy. As discussed, they make copy easy to scan. Often the designer will indicate where bullet points should be placed, but the copywriter can also make the suggestion. Here is URIM's landing page copy:

Busy as a bee? But are you as efficient?

- Get everyone in your hive working together
- Take the guesswork out of inventory tracking and planning
- Eliminate recopying and re-keying orders
- Deliver the right product to the right client, at the right time
- Spend more time growing your business!

The beehive may look like a chaotic site, but it is efficiency in motion. U-Rent-It Manager (URIM) is a party/event rental and small equipment rental order-entry and reservation system that can bring bee-like efficiency to your business.

With online inventory tracking, and sales and order calculations, URIM will have you buzzing with excitement.

Remove the guesswork

URIM takes the guesswork out of inventory tracking and planning and eliminates the need to recopy or re-enter orders. URIM includes contact manager and marketing functions and a "one-button click" to export accounting data to QuickBooks.

URIM is a cost-effective way to combat chaos and introduce order to your rental business. It saves you time and makes your hive a more productive place.

Designed with input from the party/event and small equipment rental industry, and fully supported by phone, email, and online, URIM is an intuitive application that will have you seeing positive results in hours.

Right product, right person, right time

Get the right product to the right person at the right time. Generate increased customer satisfaction and repeat business. Create more time to expand your business. Produce more honey. Now that's sweet!

Hive in Action: URIM Features and Benefits

Free Taste of Rental Manager: Download Demo

Build Your Hive: Purchase URIM

Notice the hotlinks at the end of the landing page copy. If readers want to know more, they can click on features and benefits. If they want to try the product at no charge, they can. If they want to buy, they can do that too. On the demo page, prospects find guarantees and other trust-building copy. On all the pages, they find links back to the landing page and links to all the other pages.

Here is some copy from Hive in Action: URIM Features and Benefits page:

Transform your business into a hive of productivity

"When I finally decided to update my 20-year-old 'computerized' system, I went looking for a cost-efficient, integrated rental order-entry and reservation system from a supplier who was readily available for support, if I needed it. I have found all this with URIM." - Gord Robinson, WeRentIt

With URIM in place, your business will still be a hive of activity. But all activity will be focused on meeting and exceeding customer expectations, generating repeat business, and growing your business. Use URIM to:

- Become more organized and productive, better manage workload, and keep the customer satisfied
- Reserve inventory for specific time periods
- Receive alerts if you are about to over-book items
- Reserve any special equipment needed for set-up
- Produce quotes without reserving inventory
- Convert quotes into orders with a "one-button click"
- Enter separate billing and shipping addresses on forms
- Confirm and send quotes and orders by email
- Print delivery and pick-up forms to expedite delivery
- Better manage receivables and analyze sales
- Include tax exemptions and discounts on invoices
- Calculate overall sales automatically

Free Taste of Rental Manager: Download Demo

Build Your Hive: Purchase URIM

URIM: Getting Started [Note: Takes reader to landing page]

In short, the kind of thinking that you put into your print DRM material goes into your web-based DRM landing page:

- What do people need to know before they take the action that you want them to take?
- How can you build trust and confidence?

- What kind of incentive can you offer to entice them to take action while they are on the site?

When you write for the web, you want to make it as easy as possible for readers to scan and absorb your copy. That means writing shorter sentences and paragraphs, using bold headers and bullet points when and where appropriate. (These same principles can be applied to print-based DRM brochures as well.)

Let's look at part of another landing page below, this one about media interview training. It puts a call to action for a free report close to the top of the page. This is a common landing page tactic. The free report includes practical information the reader can use, more information about the training offered, and contact information. The free report call to action on the landing page does not interfere with the overall flow of the copy (again, design and layout are as critical as the writing of copy here). Of course, the free offer is repeated at the end of the landing page as well, along with relevant contact information.

Are you ready for your interview?

You never know when a reporter will call. So be prepared. Paul Lima can have you ready in one interactive session.

Are you seeking media attention? Are journalists seeking you? Either way, you need to be prepared for interviews with journalists, because they are prepared to interview you.

Why be prepared?

It's the information age and every executive, manager, corporate spokesperson and business owner should be able to condense news, financial data, product information and other announcements into brief, convincing messages—expressed in an articulate, memorable manner.

When it comes to getting your organization's message out to the public—customers, shareholders, sponsors, donors and other stakeholders—knowing how to talk to journalists and interact effectively with the media is essential. What you say and how you say it can have a lasting impact on your business because the media helps Canadians form opinions.

Request your FREE *Are You Ready for Your Interview* report today. The report gives you practical advice to help you prepare for interviews with print and broadcast reporters. Email: info@paullima.com with "Media Interview Report" in the subject line.

The key to successful interviews?

Developing and delivering a message that is simple, interesting and newsy is key to successful interviews. In most interviews, you should stick to several carefully crafted key messages and draw on a couple supporting points and examples. You should judiciously repeat key messages for emphasis, while answering questions. Paul Lima's half-day or full-day media interview training seminars will show you how to do just that.

> "We have been using Paul Lima for media training for every client at Infinity PR. Paul's training is insightful and our clients take away great learning from the sessions. All of our clients have been extremely happy with the training." - Alan McLaren, Infinity PR

The landing page copy goes on to describe how the media training seminars can help you prepare for media interviews in one interactive session, in person or over the phone (which is how many interviews are conducted), and describes the learning objectives of the training. It also includes another testimonial, a link to an article that describes how media interview training, coupled with effective PR, turned a book into a Canadian bestseller, and contact information. Finally, it repeats the "request your free media interview training report" information.

Again, this approach puts a call to action up front. The use of bold subheads, short paragraphs, and boxes for the testimonials all make the copy easy to scan. There is no incentive to "buy" media training; however, the call to action for the free report is clearly stated, as is the contact information. The free report would be used to demonstrate the trainer's knowledge about media interviews and would include contact information and a call to action.

In summary, when writing for the web, you want copy that

- Is clear, concise, focused, well written, and easy to scan and absorb
- Speaks to a clearly defined target market
- Conveys your purpose and supports your purpose
- Presents a clear call to action and, if appropriate, an incentive to act

Generally, web copy should be more concise and shorter than print-based writing; however, you still need to capture attention, hold interest, influence attitude and ask for action. In short, web copy should not be so short that it skips any of those steps. It should also not be so concise that it leaves out important information that the reader requires before deciding to act.

Again, if you have a media release, a report, or any other long document that you want to share with website visitors, you do not have to rewrite it or format it for the web. You can post it on your website and link to it. If your site visitors need to read it, they will. But it's a good idea to include a summary of the document with your link to inform the reader about the document topic and purpose. That will help readers decide if they want to click and read. If the document is critical, consider creating a web-friendly version of it so site visitors can read it right on the spot.

Now What?

Now pick a product for which you created a DRM brochure and convert your brochure into a DRM website landing page. Once again, think hook, line and sinker. However, keep in mind that the prospect has used keywords to find you. He/she is pre-qualified—so put your call to action up-front. Don't forget to use the hotlink advantage. And write poetically, at least as we have defined it for ad copy.

Chapter 20: Search Engine Optimization

Search Engine Optimization (SEO) is the process of making a website accessible to search engines and improving its rank in search engine listings when people search for the type of information, goods, and/or services that you offer from your website. That leads to the question: How do you go about optimizing your site for the highest possible search engine rank?

A detailed answer to the question goes beyond the scope of this book. (A detailed answer is another book: *It's 11 PM. Do you know where your website ranks? How to optimize your website for the best possible search engine results.*—available online at www.paullima.com/books.) However, any copywriter working on website copy should be aware of a few basic SEO tools.

Search Engine: A website that employs 'bots to search the web and then indexes the information gathered by their 'bots in a searchable database accessible by search engine users seeking information using keywords. Based on the keyword, the search engine returns, or serves up, a list of links to web pages where the keywords were found. The rank or order in which listings are served up depends on how well the websites are optimized for search engines.

Why Optimize?

Since the web is being used for product research and comparison, comparison pricing, and to close sales, companies are doing their best to attract visitors to their websites. However, there are hundreds of millions of pages on the web, all vying for attention. While behemoth corporations such as Coke, Microsoft and Nike can draw audiences to their websites with the weight of their brand and marketing muscle, small and medium businesses draw most of their online traffic through search engines.

To show up in search engines results, a website must be submitted to the search engine, or found and indexed by search engine robots ('bots). It can take anywhere from several days to several months or longer to index a website. Proper SEO helps speed up the process.

To rank high in search engine results, the site must be optimized for relevant search terms. When it comes to search results, rank matters.

Traffic drops significantly by rank, according to the Atlas Institute, the research and education arm of Atlas DMT, an advertising technology provider. The first site listed in search engine results receives three times the hits of the fifth site; the first 10 sites (generally the first page of results) are visited 78% more often than sites listed 11th to 30th.

Keywords are Key

Before you begin to optimize a website for the best possible search engine results, you need to define your keywords and phrases—the words and phrases prospective customers will enter into search engines when looking for the kind of product or services you sell (or the causes you support, the political stance you take or the hobby you enjoy).

Once you have defined those keywords:

Use a consistent, text-based site navigation menu that incorporates your keywords. Search engines like text (content). They use site content when determining site relevancy to search terms. The 'bots the search engines send out to find websites cannot read images, so your navigational menu should ideally be composed of text. If it is composed of images (many *words* on the web are actually graphic images that spell them out), then make sure you use *alt tags* (see below).

Include keyword text tags (alt tags) with graphics (or a graphics-based navigation menu). Every image on a website has a name (something.jpg or imagename.gif and so on.). HTML code is used to display an image in a browser page (HTML code goes beyond the scope of this book). The images mean nothing to the 'bots. If you add an *alt tag* to your HTML code, then you are adding readable content that the 'bots can use.

Note: Have you ever placed your cursor over an image and seen one of those little yellow flags with text? If so, your browser is set to display alt tags and the website designer used alt tags. The 'bots pick up the alt tag as text. So your alt tag should be something like "world's greatest freelance writer"—only substitute your keywords or phrases for mine.

Combine keyword text with Flash. The 'bots cannot read Flash animation pages, so make sure you include some keyword text on a Flash-based website page.

Build a text site map, an uber-navigational page, one that includes links to every page on your site. Link to your site map from your home page so the 'bots that land on your home page can find your site map. Your site map will help the 'bots find and index every page on your site.

Write meta tags. Meta tags are embedded in HTML code and they can contain your keywords. Three basic meta tags are particularly meaningful: Title, Description and Content. Only the title tag is seen by visitors. The title meta tag displays the name of each website page in the visitor's web browser. You can change the title meta tag on each page to reflect the products, services or information on each page. You can also change the description and content meta tags, but unless each page or your site changes dramatically—golf shoes versus bridal shoes—you will most likely use one set of description and content meta tags.

Note: Although not as important to rank as they were in the pre-Google days, meta tags are read by all search engines and may be used to display information about your site in search engine results. If your meta tags are focused on your keywords, if they are all thematically related and are in sync with the content on your site, the search engine believes your site is about what it says it is about and it pays greater attention to your meta tags when ranking your site.

Use keywords in all your site content. Every descriptive paragraph on your site should include keywords or phrases. Make sure links include them too. Instead of using a link that says "Click here for information on our products" use one that includes your keywords, such as "Click here for information on RubberBand's super-durable, superior elastic rubber bands that stretch to infinity and beyond." See the difference?

What is Content?

For the purpose of SEO, content includes any text that the 'bots can capture. Images (graphics), animation and Flash are not content. In other words, words created in a graphics program and displayed on your website are not content.

How do you know what content is applicable to SEO? Go to a web page (in your web browser) and click on:

Edit > Select All > Edit, Copy

Then open Notepad (not Word or WordPerfect!) and click on:

Edit > Paste

Anything you see in Notepad (which cannot display graphic images) is editable text or content. And 'bots love content.

Beg, borrow and barter reciprocal links. When determining Page rank, most search engines look at *Link Popularity* or the number of links that point to your site (from other sites). For instance, using links from Site A to Site B as a vote by Site A for Site B, Google's PageRank system determines the value of pages and sites. Google and other search engines see links to a site as a validation of the site. The greater the validation, the higher a site shows up in search engine results (as long as it is also well optimized for keyword searches). So if you can get non-competitive sites—especially if they are industry-related sites—linking to your site, you can improve your search engine results.

Note: Do not build fake sites with keywords and create links from them to your main site. That is known as SEO spamming. If the 'bots pick up on this, and they will, your sites will be delisted from the search engine.

Consider blogging. 'Bots like content related to your search terms and they like links to your site. A "blog" (web log), if it pertains to your products or services, will contain keywords related to your products or services. If others read your blog (how you get them to do that goes beyond the scope of this book) and like what they read, they will link to your blog. So there you go: content and links! Just what you need.

Submit your site to search engines. While the 'bots may find you if you have links to your site, you should not sit back and wait. Instead, visit the major search engines and find out how to submit your site.

Consider paying for search engine ads. That deserves an entire chapter on its own—Chapter 21, in fact.

Chapter 21: Search Engine Pay Options

If you go to Google and search "Google Ads," you'll find about 117,000,000 links indexed in the Google search engine. It does not cost anything to have a web page indexed in the Google search engine. If I had information on my website about Google Ads and my site was ranked, oh, one million links down, visitors would never find my site. If I were selling the secrets of how to effectively use Google AdWords, I would not make any money.

What can I do to combat a low rank? I can set up a Google Ad (the ads appear to the right of the free, indexed links) like so:

> <u>Top Website Advertising</u>
> *www.INeedHits.com*
> Your Website found on 1st page.
> Get Your $80 Free Advertising Now!

This particular ad was listed number one when I used the search term "Google Ads." (Your search results may vary; advertisers can start and stop their Google Ad campaigns at any time.) How did the advertiser manage to get the ad listed first? He set up the ad to show up when Google visitors search for keywords related to Google Ads and he paid more per click than other advertisers who associated their ads with keywords related to Google Ads.

Fee-based Ad Options

There are many fee-based search engine listing options—more than this book can cover. Many options, like Google AdWords, are of the Pay-Per-Click (PPC) variety: You pay each time someone clicks on your ad. Others options include Pay-Per-View (PPV): You pay each time someone views your ad.

With Google AdWords you create your own ads, choose keywords to help Google match your ads to your audience, and pay only when someone clicks on your ad or ads. The more you're willing to pay and the more times people click on your ad, the higher your ad ranks. Since rank for Google Ads is a combination of the price you pay and how popular your ad is, your copy had better be effective enough to encourage clicks if you want it to rank higher than ads posted by your competition.

Let me repeat that: Your copy had better be effective enough to encourage clicks. When you place an ad on Google, you want a response—a click. In short, Google Ads are three-line direct response marketing ads with a fourth line for your URL or website name.

Yahoo! and Bing listings also allow commercial websites to run ads in their search engines. And countless websites are willing to sell you banner and text ads as well. I suspect that you can name a target market and find a website that is catering to that market. Say you want to sell a product or service to Canadian actors. Where would you advertise? Why, on Canadian Actor Online (www.canadianactor.com) of course. And on it goes.

If each PPC click or each PPV view brought you more business than the cost of the click or view, you would not care how much you had to pay per click or view. However, most views do not result in clicks and many clicks bring you tire-kickers—visitors who are browsing but not buying. Long and short of it: You want to be able to set a ceiling on what you pay, monitor results (most pay sites have reporting tools), and make marketing budgeting decisions based on results.

More About Google Ads

Google's pay-per-click AdWords are exceptionally popular. With AdWords, you get to create your ads (within space limitations), choose keywords to match ads to search terms, and you pay when someone clicks on your ad. There is an activation fee of US$10 and you can choose a maximum cost-per-click (CPC) from US$0.05 to US$50 per day.

The AdWords character (letters, symbols, spaces) limitations are strict. You cannot go over character count when you create your headline, your display URL and two lines of ad text.

Here are the maximum character counts:

Headline: 25 characters

Display URL: 35 characters
(**Note**: The destination URL—the code behind the hotlink that takes users to the actual web landing page—can be up to 1,024 characters)

Line 1: 35 characters

Line 2: 35 characters

Again, you get to link your ad to any keywords you want to. Let's look at a few Google Ads and their keywords. What happens if I search for "coffee delivery?" I see eight ads. Here are three of them:

Coffee Order
www.communitycoffee.com
Official Community Coffee Site,
Shop for coffee online and save!

Coffee Delivery
www.BizRate.com
Find Best Bargain Prices On
Fast Quality Coffee Delivery!

Coffee delivery
www.coffeefarm.com
Enjoy Specialty Coffee Delivered
Right To Your Door. Best Prices.

Now what happens if I search for "coffee delivery Toronto?" I see five ads. Some are the same as the "coffee delivery" ads, but look at this one:

Coffee Services –Toronto
www.mrcase.com
Home & Office Delivery By The Case.
Serving The GTA For Over 20 Years!

Mr. Case only delivers coffee in the greater Toronto area (GTA), so it would make no sense for Mr. Case to compete with the companies that have their ads set to appear when someone types in the keywords "coffee delivery." Instead, Mr. Case's ad is linked to the keywords "coffee delivery Toronto" to reflect the geographical area it services. And the ad copy reinforces that. It says "GTA." If you don't know what the GTA is (i.e. you do not work in the GTA), Mr. Case is hoping you will not click on the ad, because the company cannot service your coffee needs.

Presumably, the other coffee companies—the ones that show up based on the use of both keyword phrases—can service you if you are located in Toronto. If not, their ads should not show up for the "Toronto" search; it would be a waste of money if someone in Toronto clicked on the ad and could not purchase anything.

Writing Google Ads

Let's look more closely at the Mr. Case ad. What do we see? While not quite a hook, line and sinker, we do see elements of DRM advertising. The headline (Coffee Services –Toronto) speaks directly to the target market—the person who typed the search term "coffee delivery Toronto." So it captures my attention. The second copy line reinforces the delivery concept, and "by the case" gets me thinking about price—they must sell at a discount if they deliver by the case.

The third copy line builds trust by overcoming a possible objection: Who are these people? I've never heard of them. Perhaps I've never heard of them, but they have been "Serving The GTA For Over 20 Years!"

All right, then. I trust them. *Click*!

Now let's go to Google and search for something computer-oriented: contact management software. Let's look at one of the contact management software ads:

<u>Contact Mgt Software</u>
www.NetSuite.com
Fully integrated with Outlook.
30-day free trial.

Gee, isn't that headline boring. All it does is repeat the keywords. But wait a minute! What was I looking for? Does that headline not tell me that I have found exactly what I was looking for? If I use Outlook, as most businesses do, I'm interested. And hey, there's a free trial. What have I got to lose? *Click*. And I'm on the landing page, the page that then tries to sell me. We'll look at writing landing page copy in the next chapter.

In summary, you can pack a lot into a few short lines—including a hook, line and sinker. And in many ways, that's what writing for the web is all about—saying as much as you can in as few words as possible. But not using so few words that your reader misses your point or purpose and does not know what you want him or her to do.

What about this one?

<u>Contact Management</u>
www.appshore.com
Online, Easy to Use, Only $9 User
Customers Compare Us to Salesforce

Similar dull headline! But it's a hook because it too tells me that I have found what I wanted. The first copy line spells out a feature and a benefit, and manages to work in the price. Cool. And the second copy line positions the software as a substitute for Salesforce. If you know anything about contact management software, you know that Salesforce is the most popular online contact management software on the market. So in one line, David says, "I am as good as Goliath." Of course, by using the price in the previous line, the copywriter is implying that David is also less expensive.

See how you can pack a lot into a few short lines?

Now What?

With that in mind, review the ads for which you created landing pages and write Google AdWords copy. All the principles we have discussed in this book apply. You must speak to your target market using words, phrases and concepts that they can identify with, or that reflect their needs or desires. You must lure them in and cause them to act (click).

Remember that your target market has pre-qualified itself by entering keywords related to your ad—keywords that you chose to associate with your ad. They are hot prospects. Who could ask for anything more?

Now pick products for which you created a DRM landing page and create three Google Ads to lure readers to those landing pages.

Follow the Google Adsense word count. Within the limitations of that word count, capture your reader's attention with a hook, hold the reader's attention with a line, and see if you can motivate action with a sinker.

Keep in mind that your ad has appeared because the reader has used key words related to your product or service. In other words, you are dealing with a hot prospect. Motivate this person to click on your ad.

Chapter 22: Copywriting and Social Media

This book focuses on print advertisements, be they words on the page or words on a computer screen, not on audio or video promotions. With that in mind, we have to take a moment, a couple of chapters actually, to look at copywriting and social media, including blogging.

Social media websites, often called user-generated content sites, include websites such as LinkedIn, Facebook, Twitter, and blogs, as well as (but to a lesser extent) online discussion forums. YouTube is also a social media site, but it is a video-based site, so we will only mention it in passing. This chapter includes an overview of social media in general and of LinkedIn, Facebook and Twitter specifically, with a passing glance at online discussion forums and YouTube. It also looks at why companies should monitor what people are saying about them on social media channels. In the next chapter, we go blogging.

Social Media Stats

Social media has grown faster than any other media to date. For instance, it took radio 38 years to reach 50 million listeners. It took TV 13 years to reach 50 million viewers. The Internet hit 50 million surfers in 4 years.

Facebook hit 200 million users in less than a year and has now surpassed 800 million users. To put the growth of social media into context, social media has overtaken porn as the number one activity on the web, so you know there are many, many people engaged in social media.

Facebook

All of Facebook's users are on the Internet, but not all Internet users are on Facebook; however, Facebook users congregate in one place—on Facebook. Because so many people are on Facebook, advertisers want to be there too.

Facebook users tend to chat and interact socially, but the site is used for promotional purposes because it has so many subscribers. Companies run ads on Facebook and many companies have Facebook sites. In fact, some business-to-consumer companies often don't include their corporate website in ads; instead, they include their Facebook address (www.facebook.com/company-name) and try to drive Facebook members to their Facebook pages. They hope visitors will read their promotional messages and view videos, "like" their page, engage in discussion and post positive comments, enter contests, and interact in other ways the company initiates. In other words, they try to make their Facebook page "sticky"—to get visitors there, keep visitors there, and to keep them coming back.

Dove, for instance, has one million Facebook fans. On its Facebook home page (www.facebook.com/dove), the company has copy, images and links to videos. While some of the material promotes products, some of it promotes causes that the company supports. Here is part of Dove's Facebook mission, as posted on its Facebook home page: "Dove on Facebook is about promoting positive self-esteem and helping women feel good about their unique inner and outer beauty...."

On its Facebook wall, where interactive dialogues take place, Dove initiates the discussion with posts like this: Do you have sensitive skin? "Has your Dermatologist or Doctor ever recommended using Dove Sensitive Skin?" Visitors can "like" the message or respond to it, such as this reply from Alicia: "I've been devoted to Dove for over 30 years. WON'T use anything else. The sensitive skin product is awesome! Thanks."

While there is room for copywriters to produce Facebook promotions, user-generated comments represent terrific word-of-mouth promotion. Fact: 78% of social media users trust peer reviews; 14% of TV watchers trust ads. So companies want to generate positive comments on social media sites—so much so that some companies have been accused of planting comments. If that trend continues, trust will diminish. While companies that use social media need to drive their agenda, they don't want to cause people to feel that they are being manipulated—or the social media network will call companies out and generate negative publicity.

LinkedIn

LinkedIn is the world's largest business-to-business social media network, with over 100 million members and growing. LinkedIn members:

- connect with contacts in their industry
- boost brand awareness
- showcase their knowledge by exchanging ideas, insights and opportunities with professionals in their target market

On LinkedIn, you can set up a company profile and personal profiles for employees who join the site. Individuals can connect with others in their field and participate on discussion boards where their target market might hang out discussing industry-related issues.

When it comes to participating in LinkedIn, companies should set up formal accounts and determine who will set up individual accounts. Sales & Marketing often sets up the LinkedIn accounts; however, other groups (based on knowledge, experience and/or geographical location) might set up accounts too. Individual and corporate profiles on LinkedIn should be professionally written and reflect any key messages a company wants to convey about itself and its products, services and support.

Many people join LinkedIn, connect with others, or accept invitations to connect, and then do nothing. One way, however, to raise a personal or corporate profile, and build brand awareness, is to participate in discussion groups. While finding and joining various discussion groups goes beyond the scope of this book, I will say that LinkedIn makes it easy to do. The key, once you join (or start) a group, is to participate in an open manner that is not overtly promotional. Most groups are moderated, which is good because it minimizes spam posts and ensures a degree of decorum.

Companies should decide on who should join which groups, and co-ordinate action so that employees are not working at cross-purposes. Even though discussion group messages should not be overtly promotional, that does not mean a company cannot announce new products or services; it means that companies should not answer questions or address issues with overtly promotional messages. People will simply tune out such messages.

Instead, a group member should post relevant questions, answer questions posted by others, or comment on answers others give. Posting questions about issues or problems can be a good way to get discussions going. At the same time, answering questions can be an excellent way to demonstrate your knowledge about issues and situations. The poster can also include a short signature at the end of a discussion group post—name, title, company name and website address—for another subtle plug.

While this is not advertising, participating in discussion groups can demonstrate how knowledgeable company employees are about relevant issues and raise awareness about companies. With that in mind, all messages should use appropriate tone and be well written. If an issue is particularly important, the person posting a response might want to get a copywriter or editor to review and edit a message before it is posted.

By way of an aside, a Google search will reveal that there are discussion groups (or discussion forums), and sometimes many discussion groups, on almost any topic or issue. Companies should search the web and find relevant discussion groups. That doesn't mean they should join them all. Many are full of spam, flames and off-topic posts. However, many are also moderated and filled with intelligent conversations. Companies should choose which ones they want to join and participate as may be required. It can all be rather overwhelming, which is why any company, small business or independent practitioner should set priorities based on relevant opportunities to promote the company, raise brand awareness and, most appropriate in discussion forums, build credibility.

Companies can advertise on LinkedIn, as they can on Facebook. If they chose to do so, all the principles addressed in this book come into play. Ads on LinkedIn, which are similar to ads on Google, should capture the attention of a defined target market and motivate people to click. When ads are clicked on, they should lead to a landing page, not a corporate home page, that encourages visitors to take a specific action.

Twitter

Twitter has been defined as the social media networking site for those who do not have many real friends and require random strangers to know minute details of their daily lives. However, Twitter is not used solely for short (maximum 140 characters) personal comments. People comment on all sorts of topics—personal life, social situations, causes and issues, politics, celebrity gossip, products and services, and so on.

If you tweet, as posting a message on Twitter is called, nobody receives what you have to say unless they choose to follow you. How to gain Twitter followers goes beyond the scope of this book. One way, though, is to follow people who tweet about topics of interest to your company. The people you follow can then choose to follow you. (There are other ways to build your followers; a quick Google search on the topic will reveal a number of articles that may be of interest.)

Twitter has well over 100 million users, although many subscribers seldom tweet and don't regularly read tweets of those people they follow, or they tweet a lot when they join and then the novelty wears off.

So should companies join Twitter? As mentioned, there is only so much companies can do. If a company feels its target market is on Twitter, then it should consider tweeting. Companies can use Twitter to build brand awareness by tweeting about existing and new products and services. They can also use tweets to drive traffic to their websites, Facebook pages and blogs (see next chapter on blogging). For instance, a company can announce a contest on its website, Facebook page and/or blog, and can tweet about it to drive traffic to those sites. Also, if you tweet and I follow you, and I like your tweet, I can *retweet* it to my followers, many of whom might not follow you but might be interested in your information.

The Circle of Social Media

This positive cyber word of mouth can help spread your message and drive traffic to a website using what I call "the circle of social media."

I am a freelance writer, author and writing trainer. While my website, www.paullima.com, reflects that, my blog, www.paullima.com/blog, on the other hand is primarily (not exclusively) used to promote my books on copywriting, business writing and the business of freelance writing. When I create a new blog post, I post the title of the post and its website address on my Facebook page, on LinkedIn and on Twitter. That helps drive traffic to my blog, and the circle of social media is complete.

My hope then is that the informative blog post will raise my profile and make me seem like a credible author, as well as spur people to like and repeat my message. And that, I hope, will help drive the sale of my books.

YouTube and Other Social Media Outlets

Most YouTube users create and post funny, odd or quirky videos on YouTube, or post social commentaries on a variety of topics; however, many companies and individuals, such as musicians and authors, post promotional videos on the site.

Once a video has been posted on YouTube, it can be embedded in a website or blog or on Facebook, and linked to LinkedIn and Twitter. Again, the goal is to use social media (writing) to drive viewers to the promotional video and to create buzz about it.

While Lady Gaga (or her recording company) can post a Lady Gaga music video on YouTube and have over a million people view it in a matter of days, companies should not expect to reach a mass audience. And why would they want to? For the most part, companies want to reach their target market. If a video is well made (well written and well produced) and contains valuable and/or informative information, it can attract an appropriate viewership—members of the identified target market. And if viewers like it, they can embed it in blogs and on Facebook and post links to it on LinkedIn and Twitter. So YouTube can be a viable promotion vehicle.

There are many other social media sites, too many to list here. But here are several that might be of interest to companies.

Tumblr is a site that lets you share anything—text, photos, quotes, links, music and videos—from your browser, phone, desktop, email, or wherever you happen to be.

Flickr is an online photo management and sharing application. The site has two main goals: to help people make their photos available to a select or mass audience, and to enable new ways of organizing photos and video. Companies can use Flickr but, as with any marketing, they should have a concrete business reason—building brand or product awareness, raising profile, driving sales—before choosing to use the site.

Google Buzz is a social networking and messaging tool from Google, designed to integrate into the company's web-based email program, Gmail. Users can share links, photos, videos, status messages and comments organized in "conversations" and visible in the user's inbox. (Since this book was first published, Google has abandoned "Buzz" and now runs **Google+** as its social media site.)

There is a list of social media sites, and what they are about, on Wikipedia – http://en.wikipedia.org/wiki/List_of_social_networking_websites.

Wikipedia itself is a social media site, in that users generate the content on the site. In other words, companies can have Wikipedia entries on the site—entries that can be edited by anyone who has a Wikipedia account. And if people feel a Wikipedia entry is incorrect or offensive (and incorrect or offensive is in the eye of the beholder) they will alter the post.

Monitor Your Social Media Quotient

Because social media lets people comment on anything companies write, and in some instances revise what they've written, and lets people write pretty much anything they want about companies, businesses should seriously consider monitoring what others are saying about them on the web and on social media sites, and should establish a corporate policy on how to react to negative, and positive, comments.

In the age of social media, when it comes to getting your organization's message out, knowing when and how to react to good, bad and ugly tweets, blog posts, Facebook comments, YouTube videos and so on is essential. The reason? Your comments go out directly to stakeholders, unfiltered by reporters who write articles for media outlets. What you say and how you say it can have a lasting impact on your business, because social media also helps Canadians form opinions.

In social media situations, you should be prepared to convey carefully crafted key messages. But you have to realize that you will often be talking directly to your customers or prospects. If they have complaints or objectives that you cannot overcome, they will not be customers or prospects for long. And if you get into an online mud-slinging match, no matter how unfair you feel a comment was, you could be exposing the cat fight, so to speak, to the world, or at least to the world of your target audience. In short, a company should acknowledge positive comments. It should never get into an online screaming war of words (a flame war) with people who make negative comments. But it should have a policy on how to, or if to, respond negative comments and remarks.

To see what people might be saying online about your company, or any topic, you can subscribe to Google Alerts—www.google.com/alerts. Google Alerts are email updates of the latest relevant Google results based on your choice of query or topic.

Follow Paul on…

If you are interested in seeing how I use social media, which I do intermittently, I confess, you can:

- Follow me on Twitter – https://twitter.com/PaulWriterLima
- Friend me on Facebook – www.facebook.com/paul.lima
- Or "like" my Facebook fan page - www.facebook.com/pages/Paul-Lima/183948319355?ref=nf
- Subscribed to my blog – www.paullima.com/blog
- Connect with me on LinkedIn - www.linkedin.com/profile/view?id=4128829&trk=tab_pro
- View my *How To Write A Non-Fiction Book In 60 Days* YouTube trailer – www.youtube.com/watch?v=ytmUI17gtgg

Chapter 23: Copywriting and Blogs

As we know, blogs are an online phenomena, with well over 500,000,000 blogs, and growing, out there. (Even though, it must be added, the majority of these are "ghost blogs"—that is, blogs that have been abandoned in cyberspace.) And yes, many blogs are frivolous and personal; indeed, some companies think blogs are only used by people who are interested in celebrity gossip or venting about some perceived injustice.

In other words, there is a feeling that blogs are not used for business purposes. However, when it comes to blogging, you don't have to care what individuals are posting in their blogs. All you have to care about is *your* content.

Blogs that present solid business, technical or related-industry information are read on a regular basis. Company blogs may not attract a mass consumer readership, but that is not the goal of such blogs. As with other promotions, blogs should be set up to attract the attention of a defined target market, not a fractured mass audience.

Note: If you want to see how I use the content in this chapter on my blog to promote my freelance writing services—in this instance, my freelance blog writing services—without going at all hard sell, visit my *Why Blog* index page on my blog: http://paullima.com/blog/?cat=397.

There are many reasons why companies should blog and take a planned, systematic approach to producing useful, informative and compelling blog content that focuses on topics of interest to their target market.

Blogs can boost the rank of a company's website in search engine results, help companies deepen their relationship with existing customers, engage new prospects, and build their brand in the online universe.

Boost SEO

Since a website's rank in search results is determined by its relevance to specific search terms and by link popularity, blogs make sense.

As you can imagine, a company's blog posts would use the kind of keywords that its target audience might use if searching for information related to the company's products or services. If your target audience finds posts in your company blog interesting, informative and credible, they might post links on their blogs and websites to your blog posts. Over time, your company blog would use and repeat a variety of keywords and phrases relevant to your industry and would be linked to from a variety of other blogs and websites. All of this would greatly boost your company's rank in search results based on relevant keywords and phrases, which would drive even more traffic to your blog, which can be (and should be) linked to your website.

By ranking high in search results, blogs that present interesting, informative and credible information capture the attention of a defined target audience, and they can keep readers coming back. If readers find the content of a blog interesting, informative and credible, they can subscribe to the blog using an RSS feed or by email. Whenever the blog is updated, the reader is notified and can click on a link to get back to the blog and read the latest entry.

Imagine Your Target Market Seeking You Out

Imagine spending nothing but a bit of time to create compelling content about your company, your products and services, or trends and issues pertaining to your industry, and having people in your target market actively seeking out and reading this content.

That is what blogs enable you to do. And that is marketing heaven.

Ironically, however, many companies do not blog or blog erratically, or they only post blatant promotional notices in their blog. In short, they miss this simple, low-cost, and effective marketing opportunity.

To attract and hold readers, your blog posts must be interesting, informative and credible. You have to give your readers something they want to read, because it helps them learn something important, work more effectively or productively, or helps them solve problems, save time or money, discover new opportunities, or take advantage of existing opportunities.

Also, to hold the interest of your audience, you need to blog on a regular basis. Regular blogging does not mean daily, as too much information can overwhelm readers. Blogging once a week seems to work for many companies, although some companies blog several times a week or a couple of times a month.

Keep Content Short(ish)

When blogging, you want to make sure your blog posts are not too long, otherwise they will not be read all the way through. Length is relative based on the topic being addressed; however, effective blog posts tend to run 250 to 600 words in length. That does not mean they can't be longer on occasion, but they should not be much longer on a consistent basis. Or, on the other hand, if you have something lengthy to say, you can post a synopsis of the topic on your blog and link from your blog post to a web page or PDF. The most interested readers will click on the link (you should be able to measure click-throughs) and continue to read.

Build Relationships and Brand Awareness

Blogs can help business-to-business (B2B) and business-to-consumer (B2C) companies deepen their relationship with existing customers. People who buy products from companies, especially if they are complex ones, like to have their purchase reinforced. In other words, even after they buy, they like to read good news about the product—how it works and can be used.

This kind of information helps reinforces their purchase decision. With their purchase decision reinforced, they are more likely to become repeat customers and more likely to tell others about their purchase. And, as most companies know, no marketing is more cost-effective than repeat business and no marketing is more effective than positive word of mouth.

Beyond that, customers want to know that technical support is available, and blogs can be used to proactively let customers know how to resolve and avoid technical issues. The blog can also present customers with tips and techniques that help them use a company's products and services more effectively and productively, and can address big-picture industry issues and trends, positioning the company as an industry thought leader in the mind of customers.

Driving traffic to a company blog can raise the credibility of the company and boost its online brand awareness. But this doesn't amount to anything unless the company can close the sale. That is why companies include links on their blogs to specific product and contact pages.

Just as every prospect who reads ads about a company's products will not buy, not every blog reader will click on links to the company's website, but the links are there for readers who want to know more. And knowing more is the first step prospects take before they buy.

Generating Blog Post Topics

Before you write a blog post, clearly decide on your topic, which segment of your target market the post will appeal to, and what problem or opportunity you will address. Your post should stay focused on that topic, segment and issue. This might mean some prospects will not be interested in particular posts; however, if you try to be everything to everybody in each post, you will end up being nothing to nobody.

With that in mind, create some big-picture subject areas that you can blog about, including industry trends, issues and opportunities, and specific issues and opportunities for various sectors of your target audience. Then brainstorm blog post ideas or topics under each big-picture subject. Within an hour or two, you can develop a number of blog post topics—topics that will be of interest to various segments of your target market.

Once you have developed the topics, create a schedule—a list of topics, the dates you will blog about each topic, and who within your company (or outside your company, such as industry analysts or customers) will write the blog posts. And make sure any post is well edited before it goes online.

Your blog post schedule will keep you on track so that your blog has a constant flow of new and compelling content, which will help hook readers and keep them coming back. Of course, as industry issues emerge, or if you produce new products/services or revamp existing ones, you can revise the schedule and make room to cover emerging issues or to blog about your new products or product updates. Beware, however, of making your blog content overly promotional.

While you can produce solid, simple and factual descriptions about your products, I suggest you go beyond such posts and blog about industry trends and issues (this is where brainstorming topics comes into play) to demonstrate the extent to which you understand your industry. You can, or course, relate some of these issues to your products, but you don't always have to do that. Sometimes simply demonstrating an understanding of an issue or opportunity, without overt commercial overtones, helps build your standing in the industry.

How to Write Blog Posts

Blog posts generally have three sections—introduction, body and conclusion.

Introductory paragraph: The crucial part of any blog post is the introductory paragraph. It should be no more than a couple of lines and should summarize what the post is about, i.e. after reading the first few lines, readers should know what the purpose of the post is and what they will learn or discover. That will entice readers to read on.

Body: Next comes the body of the post. Different points should always be separated by paragraphs and major topic shifts should have their own subheads, as we have in this post. The subhead, in conjunction with the first sentence of each paragraph or section, should spell out the topic of the paragraph or section and lure readers into continuing to read.

Because readers scan or browse when they read online content, you'll want to keep your paragraphs short to avoid large, intimidating chunks of text. If it makes sense, add graphics to illustrate points, but don't add frivolous graphics for the sake of having images in your post.

If you want to convey a series of points, consider using bulleted or numbered lists (as in the Before You Write section of this post) because they are easier to scan and absorb than full paragraphs.

Conclusion: Finally, end your blog post with a conclusion or summary paragraph, a round-up of what you've been writing about. Or, if you've been making a case for the reader to take action, end with a call to action, a list of recommendations or a link to a follow-up web page.

Blog Headlines: Accurately Reflect Content

When creating a headline or title for your blog post, you don't need to be too creative. In fact, the more direct you are, the better the headline will be. For instance, "What happens when we drain Canada dry?" might make for a cute and effective newspaper headline, one that will cause curious readers to read the article when they stumble upon the headline. But it makes for a lousy blog headline for an article pertaining to the ecological consequences of diminishing water resources in Canada.

In other words, you want your blog headline to accurately reflect the content of your article. When your article is picked up by search engines, they will serve up your headline as the link to the blog post based on keywords used for searches. How many people would search for "What happens when we drain Canada dry?" If somebody included "Canada Dry" in a search, they would most likely be looking for information on the soda pop by the same name. People interested in environmental issues might, however, search for "ecological consequences" or "diminishing water resources" and cause the search engine to serve up a link to your aptly titled article.

So don't try to write cute blog headlines; write headlines that accurately reflect the content of your blog post.

Chapter 24: Questions to Ask a Client

If you want to satisfy your clients, you have to get into their heads and start to see the world through their eyes. That is why I start each job with questions. Probably too many, if you ask some of my clients. However, the questions make them think. And the answers help me write.

While large corporate clients often have a marketing strategy in place, or background and briefing information available, I find that small and medium companies and many non-profits are barely flying by the seat of their pants. These questions help me draw information from them. Again, that then helps me create ads—ads that speak to their target market, ads that convey their purpose, and ads that elicit the action they desire.

I don't always ask all of the questions, below, but if getting information from the client is like pulling rusty nails, I ask many of them.

For a typical copywriting job, here are some of the questions that I might ask:

- Who is the target market?
- If you could boil it down to a poster child, how would you describe that one person? Be as detailed as possible.
- Who is your best customer?
- Do you want more of him/her? If so, describe that customer.
- What would that customer have to say about you?
- Do you want a different customer? If so, who and why?
- What overall impression do you want to make?
- What do you want your readers to think? To feel?
- What is the primary action you want a reader to take?
- Where do they have to go and what do they have to do to take action?
- What incentives are you offering to motivate action?
- What's in it for your customer? Why should they care?
- What problem are you solving? How? Proof?

- How do you build credibility: warranties, guarantees, testimonials, awards, references, history?

- As anyone in sales will tell you, before you can sell anything you have to anticipate and overcome your prospect's objections. What are the main objections to the product?

- What do you say to overcome each one?

- Are you IBM, Apple, Best Buy, Radio Shack, Joe's Dollar Store?

- What phrase(s) best describes your company/product: strictly business, mostly business, business casual, casual business, way cool, totally rad? Other?

Of course, if the client has a marketing strategy, I ask to see it or to read relevant sections of the plan. The marketing strategies seldom mirror the seven-stage strategy presented in this book, but having the seven-stage plan in front of you when communicating with your client can also help you focus your conversation and questions.

When all the communicating with the client is said and done, it's still you and the blank page. At that point, limber up! Do some of the creative writing exercises presented in this book. Review and follow the writing process. Make sure you have an outline that details the copy points you want to hit, in the order in which you want to hit them. Then go forth and write.

And, if you're responsible for getting your work translated, please read the next chapter—*Ad Bloopers*.

Chapter 25: Ad Bloopers

With all the money spent on advertising and all the people involved in planning and executing ad campaigns, you would think mistakes would be minimal. And they are, when you look at the volume of ads out there. However, mistakes in translation are famous. If you ever need to have ad copy translated, test it, test it and test it. And test it again. Otherwise, your ad might end up in the Blooper Hall of Shame. It helps if you use a translation bureau or agency that specializes in advertising work.

Ad Blooper Hall of Shame

➢ Coors translated its slogan "Turn It Loose" into Spanish, where it read as "Suffer from Diarrhoea."

➢ Chicken magnate Frank Perdue's line "It takes a tough man to make a tender chicken" sounds much more interesting in Spanish: "It takes a sexually stimulated man to make a chicken affectionate."

➢ When Vicks introduced its cough drops on the German market, they were chagrined to learn that the German pronunciation of "v" is eff. In German, Vicks became the guttural equivalent of "sexual penetration."

➢ Not to be outdone, Puffs tissues tried later to introduce its product, only to learn that "puff" in German is a colloquial term for a whorehouse.

➢ The Chevy Nova never sold well in Spanish-speaking countries. "No Va" means "It Does Not Go" in Spanish.

➢ When Pepsi started marketing its products in China a few years back, they translated their slogan "Pepsi Brings You Back to Life" pretty literally. The slogan in Chinese meant "Pepsi Brings Your Ancestors Back from the Grave."

➢ When Coca-Cola first shipped to China, they named the product something that when pronounced sounded like "Coca-Cola." The only problem was that the characters used meant "Bite the Wax Tadpole." They later changed to a set of characters that mean "Happiness in the Mouth."

- ➢ A hair products company, Clairol, introduced the "Mist Stick" (a curling iron) in Germany, only to find that mist is slang for manure. Not too many people had use for the *manure stick*.

- ➢ When Gerber started selling baby food in Africa, they used the same packaging in Africa as they did in North America—with the cute baby on the label. Later they found out that in Africa, companies routinely put pictures on the label of what's inside, since most people cannot read.

- ➢ When Braniff translated its slogan "Fly in Leather," it came out in Spanish as "Fly Naked."

- ➢ When McDonald's introduced breakfasts in the U.S., the company launched a billboard campaign with the headline "Good Morning, America!" When they launched breakfast in Canada, they also used a billboard campaign with the headline, "Good Morning, America!" The billboards came down three days after they went up, at a cost of thousands of dollars flushed down the toilet.

If you don't want your message to get lost in translation, hire a reputable translator and test your message to ensure you are speaking to your target market in a language they will understand and appreciate.

Sounds a lot like what you are supposed to do with your ads, does it not? Test them before sending them out there.

What are you testing for? Well, in a way, that is what this book as been about. At minimum, you are testing to ensure your ad speaks to or otherwise engages your target market, positions your product or service properly, and achieves your objective. Anything less and you might as well burn money. Sadly, there is a lot of money-burning going on in the advertising industry.

I hope this book will help you prevent such fires.

All the best with your writing!

Chapter 26: Case Studies

Apply what you have learned in this book. Review the case studies and create appropriate ad copy for the products and services in the case studies.

Case Study #1: Salvation Charities

Salvation Charity Inc. runs the In From the Cold Shelter, a shelter for homeless people in Toronto. The non-profit agency relies on both government funds and charitable donations to run its outreach program to counsel, feed and shelter the homeless. The agency has recently launched a venture to build 120 non-profit rental units in the east end of Toronto. Government funds are meant to help the agency secure land for the housing. To complete the housing project, Salvation Charity will be seeking donations of cash, equipment and labour.

For the last nine years, Salvation Charity's main fundraising event has been a gala Casino Night and Ball, with all proceeds going to support the In From the Cold Shelter. The charity is looking to expand its base, which is mostly corporate, to get consumers and tradespeople involved in the new housing initiative.

Your job is to write copy for an ad that will run in college and university publications in Toronto, a Google Ad that will be linked to "volunteer" and related words, and a website landing page. Your goal is to attract new volunteers and donors, but not alienate the existing supporters of the charity

Background Information:

According to the City of Toronto, nearly 40,000 homeless individuals (including approximately 6,000 children) stayed in a Toronto shelter at least once last year. But advocates for the homeless say those numbers are low, because they are based on shelter use and don't take into account those who live in parks or encampments.

The Shelter, Housing and Support Division of the City provides emergency shelter for individuals and families through a system of 65 shelter locations including five city-operated shelters. Shelters are overcrowded.

Figures from the Toronto District Health Council show that more than 50% of all homeless people have a mental health problem and that 30% suffer from serious mental illness.

Case Study #2: Canadian Apple Growers Association (CAGA)

The CAGA is dedicated to the marketing of Canadian apples in Canada, the US and around the world. The CAGA also lobbies the government around issues such as marketing support, rules and regulations governing the growing, harvesting, sales and marketing of apples. In addition, the CAGA supports the betterment of the industry and its producers through research, education and communication.

The Association has a clear mandate to be the "voice" for its members at governmental affairs, on national and international bodies, and at food and horticultural trade shows.

Currently, the CAGA is trying to boost apple sales in Canada by promoting the health and nutritional benefits of eating apples. It is also working to boost exports to US markets. In the US, the CAGA is focusing on marketing types of apples that are grown exclusively in Canada, such as the Ambrosia Apple.

Your job is to write promotional copy that will boost sales in Canada. If it helps, pick one city in which to launch your advertising campaign. Your job is also to launch the Ambrosia apple in the US. The launch is scheduled for the fall, and the target is New York City.

Ambrosia Apple Background Information:

The Ambrosia Apple was developed from chance seedlings discovered in the early 1980's in BC. It is now grown in BC and Ontario, but is not grown in the USA.

The Ambrosia Apple's parents are the Golden Delicious and the Starking. Ripening in late fall, it's a quality red apple, medium to large in size, with an attractive red blush and faint stripes on a cream or yellow background. Crisp, sweet, low-acid and very juicy, with a distinct, pleasant aroma and mild flavour, the apple is excellent eaten fresh or for making fresh salads, as its flesh is slow to oxidize (turn brown).

Case Study #3: Fore.com

With the price of golf balls rising and topping out at over $75 per dozen, golf balls have become an ever more costly expense for those who love to play the game. Most golfers purchase golf balls, play with them, lose them or wear them out and replace them with expensive new balls again and again.

Fore.com is a privately held company that has been in business since 1995. Based in Markham, Ontario, Fore.com is the home of the half-priced golf ball. It sells over five million recycled golf balls each year online, by phone and mail order. Orders are shipped the day they are received and most arrive in two business days. Over 50,000 golfers in North America purchased recycled golf balls from Fore.com last year.

Golfers who buy from Fore.com enjoy the following benefits:

- Save up to 65% or more over the cost of buying new
- Choose their favourite golf balls from over 400 popular brands
- Free delivery by UPS with each rental of $100 or more (about four to six dozen balls)
- Enjoy a 100% satisfaction guarantee

Instead of manufacturing golf balls and competing against the major brands for market share, Fore.com crews recover golf balls at over 300 quality golf courses, mostly in the southwest United States. Staff then clean, sort and package the recycled golf balls and golfers get a significant break on price.

Golfers can choose from over 400 leading brands of golf balls, all sorted and packaged. Golf balls come in various grades including Mint, Grade A, Grade B, Range Balls, Refinished Balls, Coloured Balls, Ladies' Balls, Low Compression Balls and High Compression Balls.

Your job is to create Google Ads (three suggested) that will attract web surfers to the Fore.com landing page. And, of course, you need to write the copy for the landing page as well.

Case Study #4: InsureIT

Founded in 1980, InsureIT is a global leader in information technology (IT) applications, software solutions and consulting services for the life insurance industry.

For over 25 years, InsureIT's proven enterprise solutions have helped major insurance companies:

- Reduce the total cost of IT administration
- Introduce new life insurance and wealth management products to the market
- Streamline customer service and product development IT infrastructure

Industry Problem:

In the face of increased competition and in a climate of mergers and acquisitions, the life insurance industry is facing many IT operational, productivity and customer pressures. Most life insurance companies run multiple IT administration systems that do not communicate with each other. Customer queues grow and customer frustration builds as customer service representatives (CSRs) search manually across multiple systems for a variety of records on each customer, and conduct time-consuming and error-prone data entry tasks.

InsureIT Solution:

InsureIT's ConsolidationPlus system enables life insurance companies to consolidate customer data across multiple administration systems, automatically giving CSRs one view of the customer no matter which systems house their various policies. This improves productivity and customer service. Life insurance companies that invest in the InsureIT/Consolidation can maintain their investment in existing IT administration systems and remove a major customer service hurdle.

Your job is to create an ad that will run in a life insurance industry trade magazine. The magazine is read by senior executives in the industry. These executives know they have a problem, but they do not understand the technology. So you have to focus on the business case. Also, create a direct response brochure to go to these same executives (you will buy the magazine's mailing list). Since ConsolidationPlus is a high-end, multi-million dollar solution, people who read your brochure will not instantly call and order. The question is: What do you want recipients of your brochure to do?

Case Study #5: Canadian Actor Online

Founded in 1998, Canadian Actor Online (www.canadianactor.com) is a national, online educational and resource website for actors. CAO is recommended by acting teachers and coaches, AMIS, Theatre Ontario, Equity, Equity Showcase and ACTRA (the actor's union) as a reliable source of information and a great place to discuss and learn about the *biz*.

Central to the website, the *CAO Discussion Boards* are organized into over 20 forums, moderated by industry professionals who answer questions about the biz. The subscriber-based discussion forums exist to combat industry fraud, help educate actors about how to find legitimate agents, photographers and workshops, assist them in preparing for auditions, and offer advice to parents with "kidz in the biz." Site members can also discuss union issues and the politics of the biz.

CAO receives some funds from the industry, but is dependent on Discussion Board subscriptions ($30 for one year) to cover many of its costs.

Your job is to create an ad that will run in trade magazine read by actors. In addition, the CAO wants to run Google Ads and needs a landing page.

While many of the resources (articles about the biz, link to other industry-specific sites) on CAO are free, the real work on the site occurs on the discussion forums, where a nation-wide community of actors congregates. Your goal is to get people to subscribe to the CAO Discussion Boards.

Note: All the other case studies are based on simulated products, services or agencies (although the simulations are based on real products, services and agencies). CAO, on the other hand, is a real website. You can read more about it online at: www.canadianactor.com.

Chapter 27: Appendices

APPENDIX I: Deconstructing Headlines

Headline:

Take a Walk on the Mild Side

Most people think this is a headline from an ad for a mild cigarette or salsa. And that is understandable. It's actually a headline from an ad promoting a walk to help raise funds to find a cure for Alzheimer's.

Remember, the goal of the headline is to capture attention. And what is the headline playing on? *Take A Walk On The Wild Side*, a song by Lou Reed that hit the charts in the early 1970s, when Baby Boomers were in their teens and twenties. Seeing this headline, a boomer would immediately become engaged— start reminiscing about sex, drugs, rock 'n roll, and so on. Attention captured.

Seeing what the ad is about, Boomers would then start to think about their aging or possible deceased parents, and their own mortality. Now they are interested. Depressed, but interested.

The ad isn't hard sell on the idea of walking for the cure or donating money to Alzheimer's. Boomers seeing this ad will not automatically sign up to walk or donate money. However, as they see other ads for this cause, they will think about it, and maybe act. Or when a youngster knocks on their door with a pledge sheet for the walk, Boomers will most likely make a donation. So the ad is not selling. It is creating awareness about the walk, using a line that speaks directly to the target market.

By the way, the walk was sponsored by an insurance company, Manulife. Why? What do Boomers have? Children (and maybe grandchildren), homes, cars and other stuff that need insurance. Manulife is not engaged in hard sell by sponsoring this cause. All the company can hope for, by associating itself with this noble cause, is that Boomers will think positive thoughts about the company when they next think about insurance. And, just maybe, they will call Manulife to get a quote.

Headline:

Over 40? Acne Blemishes?

The target market is fairly obvious. If you are under 40, it's not you. If you are over 40 and do not have pimples, it's not you. If you are over 40 and have pimples, this headline for an adult acne medication has captured your attention.

Ads cannot be all things to all people, nor should they attempt to be. They must speak directly to their target market, which this headline does.

Headline:

They laughed when I sat down at the piano. But not when I started to play!

John Caples, a famous copywriter, wrote this headline and the ad back in the 1920s, and it's still considered a classic. In fact, it was voted the best ad headline of the 20th Century. You can see the ad and read the copy (it's a long direct response ad) online at www.powerwriting.com/caples.html. The ad is promoting the U.S. School of Music, a correspondence school for people who aspire to play an instrument, but have never learned how to do so. Targeted primarily at adults, the ad tells them they can learn to play any instrument without a teacher.

It does not try to sell the reader on buying the lessons—after all, most readers will be sceptical, even after reading this extraordinary ad. However, it asks them to send for a free booklet and demonstration lesson. (Today, it would direct them to a website for more information and a free lesson.)

If you want to learn how to play an instrument, and if you'd like to do it in the comfort of your home, what do you have to lose but the price of a stamp?

Headline: *If you are a non-drinker, you can save 20% on life insurance*

This is obvious. It is aimed a people who do not drink and want life insurance. Hey, if you don't drink and you think life insurance is a scam, then the advertiser is not interested in you. But if you don't drink and you don't have life insurance because you thought it was too expensive, let's talk. And if you do drink, then you are out of luck—unless you plan on quitting.

APPENDIX II: Promote My Apple

I suspect by now you know all you need to know before you start to advertise this apple. But just in case you don't, let's review. And remember, as you scroll through the list, knowing something doesn't mean you have to use it.

Before I advertise this apple, before I even begin to write the copy, I need to know:

- What type of apple is it?
- What does it taste like?
- How was it grown (for instance, is it organic)?
- What is it used for (eating, baking and so on)?
- Specific attributes (features) and their related benefits.
- What differentiates this apple from others on the market (USP)?
- How much does it cost?
- How is it sold (individually, by the pound or dozen, by the bushel)?
- Where can I buy it?
- Where do I go for more information?
- What is happening in the business environment that might influence the promotional message?
- Who is the target market?
  - This can be stratified, and your copy would change dramatically based on the target market. For instance, how would your copy change if you were targeting: mothers with young kids, mothers with teens, health-conscious adults (men and/or women), people on diets, institutions (schools or retirement homes), independent bakers, industrial bakers, other industrial users (companies that make apple juice, for instance) and so on?
- What is the purpose of the ad—to sell, to raise brand awareness?
- What incentives can we offer to motivate action?

APPENDIX III: Nissan Pathfinder

The poetry of this ad is established in the headline: "Rough it" and "air-conditioning" are opposites, so they belong in the same thematic set and establish the concept, which might be summed up by paraphrasing the first line—adventure made civilized.

The words in *italics* belong in the same thematic set; the underlined words, while not as obvious, also belong. For instance, a 6-disc CD Bosse audio system is rather civilized, is it not?

Headline:

If you want to *rough it*, turn off the *air-conditioning*

Body copy:

Adventure has always been *civilized* in the 2002 Nissan *Pathfinder*. Available *heated* leather seats, automatic *climate control*, and a 6-disc CD Bosse audio system help keep that *tradition* alive. And as for *power* and capability, it comes with a *250-HP V6 engine* and *All-Mode 4WD*, one of the most *advanced* 4WD systems in the world. It also won the J.D. Power and Associates Award for the "Best Midsize *Sport* Utility Vehicle in Initial Quality." So, next time you *venture* into *savage terrain*, bring some *sophistication* with you. For more information, visit a Nissan Dealership today or check out www.nissancanada.com.

Chapter 28: About the Author

Based in Toronto, Ontario, Canada, Paul Lima has worked as a professional writer and communications instructor since 1980. He is also the author of 10 books on freelance and business writing.

Paul has worked as an advertising copywriter, continuing education manager and magazine editor. Since 1988, he has run a successful freelance writing, copywriting and writing training business.

Paul writes print and web-based copy and promotional material for corporate clients. In addition, he has written about small business and technology issues for *The Globe and Mail, Toronto Star, National Post, CBC.ca*, among many other publications. For more information, visit www.paullima.com.

Other Books by Paul Lima

- *How to Write a Non-fiction Book in 60 Days*

- *Harness the Business Writing Process*

- *Everything You Wanted to Know About Freelance Writing...*

- *Copywriting That Works: Bright Ideas to Help You Inform, Persuade, Motivate and Sell!*

- *Do You Know Where Your Website Ranks? How to Optimize Your Website for the Best Possible Search Engine Results*

- *(re)Discover the Joy of Creative Writing*

- *How to Write Media Releases to Promote Your Business, Organization or Event*

- *Build a Better Business Foundation: Create a Business Vision, Write a Business Plan, Produce a Marketing Plan*

All books are available in print and PDF format; many are available for Kindle Reader and ePub readers: **www.paullima.com/books**

Lightning Source UK Ltd.
Milton Keynes UK
UKOW06f2342160914

238712UK00013B/745/P